THE DREAM OF THE RED CHAMBER

A Critical Study

Jeanne Knoerle, S. P.

THE DREAM OF
THE RED CHAMBER

A Critical Study

FOREWORD BY LIU WU-CHI

Indiana University Press / Bloomington & London
for the International Affairs Center

TO MY MOTHER

Contents

Acknowledgments

FOR permission to reproduce throughout this book illustrative passages quoted from their English texts of *The Dream of the Red Chamber* my thanks to Mr. Jacob Steinberg of Twayne Publishers, Inc., publisher of the translation by Chi-Chen Wang, and to Pantheon Books, A Division of Random House, Inc., publisher of the translation by Florence and Isabel McHugh from the German translation by Franz Kuhn.

While it is always impossible to acknowledge adequately the assistance that one has received throughout the course of research and writing, I would like to pay particular gratitude to Dr. Liu Wu-chi for his support and direction, and to Dr. Norbert Fuerst, who was instrumental in the development of the manuscript.

I am most grateful to Edith Greenburg Albee of the Indiana University Press for her suggestions and encouragement, to Pamela Scheinman for her help in my revision of the manuscript, and to Sally Neylon and Linda Bippen for their editorial assistance.

Preface

PROBABLY THE most popular of the Chinese novels
read by English-speaking people, *The Dream of the
Red Chamber* has been the subject of many studies,
but the novel in its entirety has not been analyzed according to modern literary criteria. This approach
would seem most meaningful to the Western reader,
especially to one whose only access to the novel is in
translation, and who wishes to appraise the work as a
whole. The object of this study is not to conclude
whether this is a *good* novel or a *bad* novel. Rather, the
study will attempt to isolate the elements of structure
and technique that have gone into its making, examine
them in terms of carefully defined principles and then
replace them within the context of the book. Aside from
the fact that this method of analysis is already somewhat
familiar to the Western reader, and therefore seems sensible, there are several other critical justifications.

First, no comparable system of literary criticism has
developed in China, nor is literary criticism accorded the
recognition as a genre it is given in the West. Most critical statements are made in notes, letters, reports of
conversations and prefaces—in an informal and unsys-
tematic way. Part of the reason for this difference lies in
the absence of a Chinese counterpart for the Aristotelian
method of analyzing existing works of literature in order
to abstract from them basic criteria for a critical scheme
or "Poetics." More to the point, the Chinese response to

literature is intensely *personal,* and at the same time, apt to be based on non-"literary," that is, non-aesthetic, judgments. The work of critics like Lu Chi (261–303) and Liu Hsieh (fl. 530), who strove to introduce order into the critical chaos, illustrates this argument. Instead of isolating generalized critical principles, they concentrated on describing the beauty of the language and the emotional impact of particular works, on studying the intensity of emotion which produced them, and on placing them in some sort of continuum of excellence premised on their moral soundness—e.g., the ability of the work to move the reader toward or indicate to him a proper mode of action. Typically, Chinese scholarship involved establishing the authentic text of a work and analyzing its biographical, sociological and political implications. The surge of critical activity stimulated by the popularity of the vernacular novel in the seventeenth and eighteenth centuries tended to entrench this method.

A second assumption underlying this study is the compatability of the themes of *The Dream of the Red Chamber* with a Western sensibility. The variety of human beings and situations, and the treatment of universal experiences such as the "love triangle" and the "decline and fall" of a wealthy and politically prominent household, extend the novel beyond the limits of manners or its particular historical setting. The author displays an incisive psychological understanding, in marked contrast to so many of the Chinese writings riveted in folk tradition which set forth a narrow, stereotyped view of historical or religious figures. It is this quality which is the basis for the opinion expressed by C. T. Hsia, noted Chinese-American critic and author, that it is "the only work of Chinese fiction that invites valid comparisons with the tragic masterpieces of Western literature."

In Western criticism, where there *is* a strong and sys-

[x]

tematic tradition of aesthetic principles of analysis, a problem exists in the failure of critics to agree on the simplest of definitions. Even the fairly recent term "novel" is in dispute. Terms used commonly by one critic do not mean precisely the same thing when used by another, and a comparison of apparently similar statements by several critics tends to overlap and blur rather than clarify meanings. This study must, then, at the outset present a set of critical definitions which seem valid, drawing upon English and American critics. These definitions will represent a synthesis of critical thought. Where appropriate, the remarks of critics will be paraphrased to minimize the number of quotations and to eliminate critical jargon.

The diffusiveness of Western literary criticism suggests a third justification for using a synthetic method. There seems to be little danger of distorting the intentions of individual critics by applying their statements to the Chinese novel, in that each critic has attempted to arrive at a generally valid definition within the context of his own subject.

As the study will necessarily draw on the body of Chinese thought and culture, this analysis will be based on common concerns of Western and Chinese critics, among them the social and moral issues in the novel. As a result, the study will not only compare Western critics, but also will involve an historical overview of fiction in both China and the West.

The problem of identifying the female characters, whose names are translated differently in each of the English versions, has been solved by transliterating all of the names. A list has been included on page 157 for easy cross-reference to both translations. Since the male names have already been transliterated in both versions, they are not included in the list. All spellings are based on the Wade-Giles romanization system, which may lead to a few incidental differences in the transliteration of the male names, generally adding the apostrophes and diacritical marks characteristic of that system of romanization. For instance, Pao-yu becomes Pao-yü, Chin Chung becomes Ch'in Chung, etc. *Where female names occur in quoted passages, I have taken the liberty of changing their names to the transliterated version* (see list on page 157) *for greater consistency in this study.*

Foreword

THE STUDY of *The Dream of the Red Chamber (Hung-lou meng)*, which continues to attract critical attention today in China and abroad, has acquired a designation of its own: *Hung-hsüeh*, or "Red-ology." No other Chinese novel at any period of China's long literary history has aroused such an immense interest in scholarly communities as this mid-eighteenth century novel by Ts'ao Hsüeh-ch'in, the impoverished scion of a once wealthy official family. Since the beginning of this century, many decades of indefatigable Chinese scholarship have produced a wealth of information on *The Dream of the Red Chamber* that aids greatly in our understanding of the novel.

Most noteworthy for scholarly research is the discovery of at least six handwritten, annotated copies of the novel, variously dated from 1754, when the author was still living, to 1784, seven years before the novel's first publication. While some of these copies are fragmentary, others contain intact the first eighty chapters, presumably all that Ts'ao Hsüeh-chin left at the time of his death. The fact that there are preserved today so many handwritten copies of Ts'ao's manuscript (itself irrevocably lost) suggests the extensive interest in the novel among those of Ts'ao's contemporaries who had heard of the work and were anxious to obtain personal copies prior to its publication. The innumerable commentaries, often candid and revealing, were written by Chih-yen Chai (a pseudonym, literally, "the studio of the rouge inkstone") and several others, all of whom appear to be familiar with the author's life and work. These annotations are invaluable in our understanding of the artist's creative process, and of the autobiographical nature of the novel. They also illuminate the structure and possible ending of the work as Ts'ao Hsüeh-ch'in originally conceived it.

Another important discovery, in 1959, was a handwritten copy of the complete 120-chapter novel (published in facsimile in 1963), said to have been transcribed during the Ch'ien-lung period (1736–95) and very likely an earlier version than the first printed edition. Most significantly, the manuscript, which bears the marks of extensive changes and revisions, was once in the possession of the editor of the printed novel, Kao Ê, who may also have been the author of its last forty chapters. Except for the words, apparently in Kao's handwriting: "Read by Lan-shu," that appear conspicuously at the end of chapter seventy-eight in cinnabar ink, there is little in the manuscript to indicate Kao Ê's relationship to it. (Lan-shu was Kao Ê's "style name.") It is uncertain whether Kao read through the entire 120-chapter manuscript and how much of it he actually used in collating and editing the printed version. This 120-chapter copy as well as the Chih-yen Chai versions provide rich materials for students of the novel.

A major effort in Red-ology is the search for source materials connected with the author and his family. Here, the successes are somewhat limited—the historical documents, imperial edicts, family genealogies, and literary works that have been unearthed relate mostly to Ts'ao Hsüeh-ch'in's ancestors and friends, but very little to Ts'ao Hsüeh-ch'in himself, the facts of whose life are still obscure. As a result of these discoveries, we can now establish the date of Ts'ao's death as 1763 or 1764, but there is still no consensus of critical opinion as to his birth date: 1715 or 1716 seems to be the year preferred by scholars, but the date has been placed as late as 1723. It is known that Ts'ao Hsüeh-ch'in's grandfather was the well-known official-scholar Ts'ao Yin (1658–1712), whose life has been studied in some detail, but we are not sure whether Ts'ao Hsüeh-ch'in's father was Ts'ao Yin's blood son Ts'ao Yung, who died early in his twenties in 1714, or Ts'ao Yin's nephew and adopted son Ts'ao Fu, with whom the young Hsüeh-ch'in grew up. The latest view, based upon a newly discovered genealogical chart of the Ts'ao clan, seems to hold that Hsüeh-ch'in was Ts'ao Fu's son rather than the posthumous son of Ts'ao Yung, but the question is still controversial, as are the details of the novelist's life.

While Chinese scholars have contributed to the research of the novel, they have also left a maze of bewildering scholarship and fantastic interpretations that obscure the meaning of the novel. Strangely enough, this great novel has never been seriously and extensively studied as a work of literature. There are, of course, a few exceptions such as Wang kuo-wei's (1877–1927) perceptive article on the aestheticism of Ts'ao's novel, but this pioneering effort has not been continued by later scholars, who, following Hu Shih's (1891–1962) example, are interested mainly in textual and historical research. Among the many reasons for the failure of Chinese critical efforts, one important factor seems to be that the Chinese, because of their traditional disdain for fiction as a literary genre, have not fully developed a set of critical principles for such a study. In general, most of Chinese literary criticism tends to be impressionistic and metaphorical. It is here that the Chinese have much to learn from the West, and this study of *The Dream of the Red Chamber* by Sister Jeanne Knoerle, an American scholar versed in the Chinese novel, should usher in a new era of Red-ology in the East and West.

The critical approach used by Sister Jeanne is that of the comparatist: the application of Western novelistic criteria to a major Chinese novel. It is a total approach, an over-all view and analysis of the various aspects of the novel: its structure, actions, and characters; its treatment of time and space; its moral and aesthetic patterns. In this connection, one sometimes wonders whether this kind of comparative study is valid in view of the wide differences in social and cultural backgrounds between traditional China and modern West; to be more specific, whether a unique work such as *The Dream of the Red Chamber*, so highly acclaimed by native critics, will lend itself to minute critical analysis according to Western standards. For students of Chinese and comparative literature, Sister Jeanne's answer to this question could be revealing, and the result of her exploration, rewarding. But, without venturing an opinion, I will say here, in the good, old tradition of Chinese storytellers, "Reader, if you want to know what the answer is, read the book itself."

LIU WU-CHI

Bloomington, Indiana
July 27, 1972

THE DREAM OF THE RED CHAMBER
A Critical Study

(I)

Introduction

THE *Dream of the Red Chamber*, generally thought to have originated in the 1750's, has a long and complicated history with many unanswered questions concerning its origin, authorship, and autobiographical significance. The story of a prominent joint family, the Chia clan,[1] it is an enormous, complex work with social, political and philosophical implications pertinent to Chinese tradition of that period.

The novel has been translated into English twice, once by Florence and Isabel McHugh from a German translation by Franz Kuhn (hereafter referred to as the Kuhn edition), and again by the Chinese-American scholar Wang Chi-chen.[2] Neither the Wang nor the Kuhn translation is complete: both include more of the earlier chapters of the novel. Wang gives only brief summaries of the last forty chapters, while the Kuhn version abridges the latter portion of the book considerably.

There are a number of critical problems concerning the authentic and complete text of the book. The entire novel, 120 chapters in all, contains over four hundred characters and countless episodes, all in some way related to the Chia clan. Several handwritten manuscripts, the longest containing eighty chapters, are also extant, but none of them is complete. Scholars are divided on the question of authorship.

It has been traditionally argued that the first eighty chapters were written by Ts'ao Hsüeh-ch'in (1724?–1764, who died leaving the manuscript incomplete), and that the last forty chapters were the work of Kao Ê, the "editor" of the 120-chapter version that appeared in 1792. This view is widely accepted by such scholars as Hu Shih, Yü P'ing-po, Chou Ju-ch'ang and most recently by Wu Shih-ch'ang, although there are numerous disagreements among them regarding the nature and quality of Kao Ê's supplement. In 1961 Shih-ch'ang Wu published *On The Red Chamber Dream*, in which he traces the family history of Ts'ao Hsüeh-ch'in and the probable origins of the novel. This evidence, summarized also in Wang's introduction, is given here briefly: The author came from a wealthy bannerman family; the bannermen, families who had surrendered to the Manchus prior to 1644 (the year the Manchus became the rulers of China), owed hereditary military service to the Manchus, in return for which they enjoyed appointments to imperial offices and certain social privileges. The founder of the Ts'ao family was made superintendent of the Imperial Silk Industry in Nanking, an extremely lucrative post that was held by the family members from 1663 to 1728. The author's grandfather, Ts'ao Yin, a poet, playwright and collector of rare books, inherited the office. He had grown up with members of the Imperial family whom he later entertained lavishly on visits to his home, along with his many literary friends. When he died in 1712, Ts'ao Yin left behind enormous debts, which ordinarily would have bankrupted and disgraced the family. The Emperor interceded, however, appointing Ts'ao Yin's son to the same silk industry post in Nanking and Ts'ao's brother-in-law Commissioner of the Salt Monopoly at Yangchow (a position so lucrative that it was given out only for a one-year term) in order that the family might discharge their debts. Ts'ao's son died three years later (after Ts'ao Yin's own death), and the author's father, Ts'ao Fu, was made heir by posthumous adoption so that he might inherit the superintendency of the Silk Industry. In 1728 the family moved to Peking, where they lived in greatly reduced circumstances. Their sudden fall is a mystery, but Professor Wu speculates that the new Emperor probably dismissed Ts'ao Fu from office and confiscated the family properties. The records of the family end shortly after 1735, the year when the succeeding ruler reinstated a relative into the Ministry of the Imperial Household.

The Dream of the Red Chamber, an autobiographical novel, was probably written during this period in Peking by an embittered Ts'ao Hsüeh-ch'in, whose adult life was spent living in poverty far from the barely-remembered luxury of his youth. From correspondence between Hsüeh-ch'in and a friend, it appears that shortly before his death Hsüeh-ch'in lost his son, and that he left a "new wife" when he himself died after a long illness in 1764, unattended by a doctor. Supposedly he wrote eighty chapters that he circulated in handwritten manuscripts among his friends, and one or more of these manuscripts fell into the hands of professional copyists. Commentary was offered by "Chih-yen Chai" (unknown, but perhaps a close relative) whose name has become the generic term for these early handwritten manuscripts.

In 1792 the Kao Ê edition appeared with two introductions, one by Ch'eng Wei-yuan, who probably financed the publication, and the second by the scholar Kao Ê, descendant of another prosperous family. It is on evidence from these introductions that the theory of dual authorship is based. Critics tend to think that the last forty chapters are of markedly poor literary quality, which they suspect proves that Kao Ê completed the novel on his own inspiration, giving it, for example, a happier ending than was originally intended by his allowing Pao-yü to pass the Imperial Examinations.[3]

Another group of scholars, represented by Bernhard Karlgren, Lin Yu-t'ang and Chao Kang, contends that the linguistic and literary unity of the book indicated that it is mainly the work of Ts'ao Hsüeh-ch'in and that Kao Ê merely emended and redacted the last forty chapters from manuscripts available to him.

The present study upholds the theory of dual authorship, but accepts the novel, for purposes of analysis, as a unified whole (since it is generally read that way). Certain attitudes and insights can come only from reading the novel in Chinese, particularly because the translations are abridged; but wherever possible the commentary will be directed to the two translated versions, in order that the study have meaning for all English-speaking readers of the novel.

To begin with we shall place the novel in the perspective of its time and in the history of Chinese literature. Ts'ao Hsüeh-ch'in lived at the height of the Ch'ing (Manchu) Dynasty (1644–1911), a period in China's history when, after more than a century of peace, the country had reached its greatest territorial extent, its largest population and a widespread material prosperity.[4] Having swept down upon China to establish their rule as an alien tribe, the Manchus introduced little change in Chinese culture. Rather, for reasons of political expediency, they strove to maintain cultural orthodoxy, placing great emphasis, for example, on the Civil Service Examination —through which the ambitious scholar, if he followed a well-defined curriculum, might succeed to prestige, power, and wealth. These examinations represented a long tradition of drawing the most talented into the ranks of the ruling dynasty and thereby sapping any revolutionary potential in the noble families by making them servants of the state.

Those families whose members were appointed to public office held powerful positions within Ch'ing society, since many of the offices, in addition to the prestige attached to them, yielded huge profits. Polite society of the period was newly and self-consciously affluent, and the tendency was for it to become mannered—that is, excessively intent on ceremonial and conspicuous spending.[5] Confucian teaching provided the basis for an elaborate code of familial obligations and household duties, centering on the education of the young, ancestral offerings, and burial rites; thus, the fulfillment of each duty became an excuse for ostentation and formality. This was also a period of great productivity in the arts, and the wealthy families, with their intimate knowledge of traditional Chinese culture, continued to be acclaimed both as patrons and as men of letters.

The literary tradition in China was from its beginnings strongly didactic in tone, partly in its original conception, but more generally in its interpretations. Very early in the history of this culture even the most beautiful lyric poetry was interpreted moralistically, and the prose forms settled more and more into an orderly and balanced expression that reflected the Confucian values imposed upon it. Though there was no doubt a constant peasant tradition of free vernacular storytelling, the earliest examples of fiction that have reached us are the short anecdotes embodied in the philosophical or historical works of the early writers of the Han and pre-Han times. Since these writings were for and by the literati in the terse classical language that was the only written medium of the time, we do not find the spontaneity that we commonly associate with early Western fictional efforts. Instead we find a continuing and patterned use of the brief story told, not for its own sake, but to illustrate some ethical or philosophical truth. Echoes of this very strong parable-like tradition are still

[7]

extant in the search by many modern Chinese critics for symbolic, moralistic or allegorical meanings even in very lengthy pieces of modern fiction. The tradition of art-for-art's-sake, though it existed among some of the freer Taoist writers of some periods of Chinese history, has never been characteristic of Chinese artists and certainly not of Chinese critics.

We find the early roots of Chinese fiction, then, very strongly moored in the developing Confucian tradition, limited by the kind of written expression available, and fairly static and sparse during the long centuries between the Han and T'ang dynasties. With the burst of creativity during the T'ang period and later, however, more sophisticated and complex forms developed and we begin to see a two-fold and mutually beneficial tradition of classical and vernacular storytelling.

Whereas the earlier practice of storytelling had been a cognate of the historical and/or philosophical writing of the time, literary tales of the T'ang period stand on their own as interesting and valuable pieces of art, though they were still always expected to teach a moral lesson. The men of letters of this period wrote simple and independent tales and stories, especially about marvelous events, in an attempt to perfect their prose style and to capture the excitement and gaiety of this very rich and glittering period of Chinese history. These tales of the marvelous, which came to be known as *ch'uan-ch'i,* always were written in the strictly classical mode by the scholars who congregated in the capital of Ch'ang-an and who were therefore highly sophisticated themselves and writing for a highly sophisticated audience. Because of their origin and acceptance, these stories flourished for over a century, during which time they contributed to the perfecting of a simple, moving, unembellished prose style, which later converged with the developing ver-

[8]

nacular prose and found an outlet in some of the eighteenth century novels, especially *The Dream of the Red Chamber*. The inclusion of more and more elements of realism within these stories, and in the tales of love and chivalry which were also popular at the time, brought the two traditions—of classical and vernacular tales—into greater harmony and paved the way for the eventual acceptance of both modes by the highly critical Confucian Chinese of later decades.

Probably the greatest single force in the development of the second tradition, that of the colloquial tales (which paralleled and eventually outstripped the development and diversification of the literary tales) was the Buddhist influence in T'ang times. Monks became adept at reciting Buddhist stories in the temple courtyards and on the streets, and they developed highly effective and dramatic ways to hold the attention of their audiences as long as possible. These men substituted for formalities and structures of classical language such devices as suspense, dialect, wit, colorful and colloquial language, depending for success on the applause of an unlettered audience rather than the approval of the highly critical literati. By frequently interspersing songs with their recitations, they developed a kind of literary and dramatic crossbreeding that has enriched the Chinese fictional tradition up to modern times. This oral recitation of religious stories eventually branched out to include secular ballads and tales and became the precursor of the highly developed storytelling of the Sung dynasty.

By Sung times the Buddhist influence had been dissipated and Buddhist monks forbidden to tell stories publicly. The art they had developed and passed on, however, was by then well established; lay storytellers had become so popular that they organized themselves into a number of guilds and performed in tea houses and market places. To help them refresh their memories and keep themselves alert during the sometimes very pro- tracted recitation of their stories, they prepared outlines to remind themselves of the major developments of the story and of the key dialogue. These outlines, called *hua- pen*, eventually came to be recorded and passed on, much as the stories told by the Buddhist monks had earlier been recorded in a form called *pien-wen*. The greater maturity and smoothness of the *hua-pen*, however, shows the continuous development of the colloquial language since T'ang times.

These *hua-pen* follow a general pattern, opening with a preamble to whet the appetite of the audience and combining dialogue passages and comic portions in vivid colloquial style with poems and songs in the more liter- ary mode. The breaks in the story allow the narrator to take refreshments, collect money for further recitation, or encourage listeners to come back for the next day's continuation. That these promptbooks were only the bare bones of most of the stories, however, is obvious, though a few, such as "The Oil Peddler" and "The Pearl- Sewn Shirt," are fully developed and transmitted pieces of fiction.

The Sung storytellers created and developed a rich variety of stories—realistic, historical, supernatural, reli- gious—which provided a wide palette for writers in the Yüan period to use in the development of their dramas. During the even later Ming period, writers of the first long novels in Chinese history drew on these same Sung stories. The Yüan period figures only indirectly in the development of Chinese fiction, since there were no new fictional forms that came into being during this period (though there was a continuing production of stories and tales). The predominant literary expression of the period was the drama, however, and many of the stories and plots of the T'ang and Sung periods found their way into dramatic form, embellished with songs and poetry and further colloquial dialogue, which enriched the reservoir of material from which later novelists could draw.

Although the early sprawling novels of the Ming period, loosely threaded together around a basic theme, are essentially collections of stories used by the Sung storytellers and the Yüan dramatists, the influence of historical writing is strong in the development of the Ming novel.

While the colloquial short story stems directly from the oral tradition, the colloquial novel is additionally tied to the tradition of historiography. So strong is the latter influence that many Ming historical novels could be considered works written in conscious reaction against the oral tradition, . . . If the storytellers achieved the immediacy and amplitude of realism, they were at the same time vulgar didacticists interpreting history and legend in strict accordance with the concept of moral retribution. . . . Turning against this simplistic attempt to rectify the injustices of history, the compilers of better historical novels were more inclined to follow the official historians and to share their Confucian view of history as a cyclic alternation between order and disorder, as a record of the careers of great men engaged in a perpetual struggle against the periodically rampant forces of anarchy and sensuality. They show a greater respect for fact so that, while they lack the narrative amplitude of the oral storytellers, they are able to convey a sense of complex reality less circumscribed by a rigid moralism. . . . Next to the oral storytellers, therefore, the historians provide the most important literary background in the making of the Chinese novel. Until the novelists became more proficient in the arts of fiction, their reliance on dynastic histories assured them of an abundant supply of characters and events whose reality could be suggested even in a bald narrative of little artistry.[6]

The earliest and among the greatest of the Ming novels, *The Romance of the Three Kingdoms* and *The Tale of the Marshes*,* both illustrate this dependence upon history. The first of these is a straightforward chronicle of the exciting period of history when the three kingdoms of Wei, Wu and Shu Han were battling for supremacy. Written in the literary language (rather than in the already popular colloquial), the novel is part history and part fiction; but the exploits of its heroes are told with facile imagination and with a kind of immediacy of action and insight that draws the reader directly into the period and gives to these successive historical events a kind of episodic unity. This loose, episodic use of events is characteristic of the novels of both the Ming and Ch'ing dynasties, though the manner in which the episodes are related differs. In *The Romance of the Three Kingdoms* history provides an obvious tie, whereas in *The Tale of the Marshes*, though the theme centers around a historical period (medieval China of the twelfth century), the episodes simply tell the history of the 108 bandit-heroes; and except for the theme of bandit camaraderie there is almost no attempt at unification.

In *The Tale of the Marshes* the folk traditions which provoked the novel are rich and varied.

The references to Sung Chiang in formal history . . . are very sketchy and little is known of him and his group.

The folk storytellers, on the other hand, had been active in building up and expanding the legends of the Mount Liang bandit-heroes. The stories of their exploits may already have been widely known among the people in the last years of the Northern Sung dynasty, but it was in the Southern Sung that the storytellers began to spin the yarns of these brave outlaws. About the same time artists sought to portray their likenesses

*This novel has been translated also under the title *The Water Margin*.

in pictures, which unfortunately have been lost. As mentioned previously, Yuan dramatists further enriched the legends in a number of plays. Out of this vast reservoir of material emerged the novel, *The Tale of the Marshes.*[7]

Such a background provided the Ming novelists with a wide expanse of material from which to choose. Their greatest talent lay, however, not in selection but in inclusion, for the great novels of China all suffer from size, and—unlike the picaresque novels of the West—seem not to be limited to relevant material or centered around a major hero.

So far little has been said about authorship of these novels; indeed, speaking about authorship of any early Chinese novels or stories is difficult because little is known of the individuals who gave birth to them. As is obvious from what has already been written, the early tales and stories began with an oral, folk tradition in which the individuality of authorship is lost and, since the early novels were drawn largely from this tradition and from the historical chronicles, we must speak of their authors rather as editors or compilers. Without going into the enormous questions which surround the problem but which concern us here very little, we can accept Lo Kuan-chung as author-compiler of *The Romance of the Three Kingdoms;* he, as well as Shih Nai-an, a lesser-known literary figure, are given credit for putting together the legend of *The Tale of the Marshes.* At any rate, both of these works are rich in the fertile traditions of storytelling which spawned them.

Though we have mentioned only two early Ming novels, this period produced many more, often of inferior quality, with these two generally accepted as the only major creations of the early Ming period. As the dynasty wore on, however, the number and quality of full-length novels increased, primarily because the social conditions of the time had changed sufficiently to allow greater acceptance of the novel as a piece of literature. Previous to this time, and on a lesser scale into the twentieth century, the only literary works fully acceptable to the Chinese scholarly class, which controlled the critical evaluation of literature, were those works written in the classical language and in classical form. Because novels had originated in the folk tradition without the official "seal of approval" of the literati, they were never considered part of the literary inheritance and hence never given serious critical attention or comment. Evidence indicates, however, that the members of the scholarly class not only read them for pleasure but often turned a hand at writing them, although they never were incautious enough to claim their authorship. It was only as the southern cities gradually became the centers of the book trade, following the expansion of printing and publishing during the Sung-Yüan periods, and after the Mongol conquest, which broke down much of the political and hence literary influence of the scholar class, that an urban middle class with the ability and leisure time to read brought greater legitimacy to the novel and short-story forms. Though still considered inferior, the very bulk of fictional writing called for greater and greater attention and it was during the period of the late Ming and early Ch'ing that the four greatest Chinese novels came into being: *The Journey to the West* (translated in a popular, abridged version as *Monkey*), *The Golden Lotus*, *The Scholars*, and *The Dream of the Red Chamber*.

The first of these, apparently written by a scholar named Wu Ch'eng-en, tells the fanciful story of the monk, Hsuan-tsang, his early life, and his journey to get the Buddhist sutras in the West. He is accompanied by three disciples, all animal spirits—Monkey, Pigsy and

Sandy—and the story of their journey, which constitutes the bulk of the novel, is filled with action, wit and fantasy. The imaginative accounts of the adventures of the group flow directly from the folk storytelling traditions where, as mentioned previously, vivid action and clever dialogue were necessary to keep the audience's attention. Though the novel in its entirety includes many repetitious adventures and would seem overlong to most Western readers, it sustains a high level of comic spirit throughout and stands equal to any of the best-known comic novels of the Western tradition.

The Golden Lotus is considered by some critics to be the greatest of the Chinese novels, though its blatant pornography has always stood in the way of its full critical acceptance. As an example of an increasing emphasis upon realism and exactness of detail it has been called a naturalistic novel, though there has been no further broad development of this form in Chinese fiction. The unidentified author borrows from numerous sources, particularly songs and poems of the time in the classical idiom, to create the story of Hsi-men Ch'ing, an amorous apothecary who rises to wealth and power and whose descendants, not he, feel the retribution for his immoral life. Less episodic and more centralized in form than some of the other novels of the time, it probably comes closest to *The Dream of the Red Chamber* as a realistic portrayal of family life and corrupt society.

The third of the four works, *The Scholars*, written by Wu Ching-tzu, is a collection of satirical stories, loosely linked together, about various members of the scholar class. The greatest contribution of this novel to the fictional tradition of China is its total independence of the literary language and its complete integration of all portions of the story (including the usually stock descriptive phrases generally classical in origin) into the vernacular language. In this aspect, *The Scholars* is farther advanced than *The Dream of the Red Chamber*, which still makes fairly extensive use of the formalized literary language to describe the physical attributes of characters while using the vivid colloquial language to bring their actions and dialogue to life.

Thus we see *The Dream of the Red Chamber* embedded in a literary tradition which was both highly conventional and richly diverse. Because of the dominance of Confucianism, which valued uniformity, the meaning of symbols at that time tended to be expected and superficial; little thought was given to ideas, actions, or values which fell outside of those that could be absorbed by the Confucian ethic. This tendency to rigidify found a ready outlet in the written language and in literary forms which were under the supposed tight control of the most literate class in Chinese society. However, the natural buoyancy of the folk spirit of China has always lain just beneath the surface, bubbling up and overflowing during many periods throughout the long course of Chinese literary history. This earthy folk spirit, which had for long years been actively producing a bold and vibrant para-literary or extra-classical tradition during the T'ang to Yuan periods, and its mixture with the more lofty erudition and balanced formality of the Ch'ing period provided the unique soil to produce such a novel as *The Dream of the Red Chamber*.

In the long history of Western literature the novel is a comparative newcomer; it is generally considered to have been fathered in its modern form by *Don Quixote* and to have reached artistic fullness in the Russian and French novels of the nineteenth century. Criticism of the novel lagged behind its more creative progenitor; and English criticism of the novel as a technical form first claimed attention only during the latter half of the nineteenth and early part of the twentieth centuries, notably with the prefaces and critical writings of Henry James, who was much influenced by Flaubert and other French writers. Yet there has been no consensus of critical opinion outside of a rough grouping into "schools" of criticism: "Jamesians," "the new critics," the "Freudians" among others; members of these groups, while sharing a similar approach, do not necessarily consider themselves in agreement on specifics, or for that matter, recognize their own membership in a given "school."

The critical terms which form the framework for this study are *subject, story, plot* and *character*. These elements are incorporated in the total scheme of the book, its *structure*. The exact relation of the terms, however, is a matter of speculation. In proceeding to an examination of individual terms we will attempt to deal with the interrelations between some of these terms and to construct a theoretical hierarchy.

Percy Lubbock claims that a novel cannot take shape without a subject ("one and whole and irreducible") which he sees as separate from the story (although some confusion arises out of his use of the two terms interchangeably).[8] The subject, he suggests, should conveniently fit into a phrase of no more than ten words. He seems, as James did before him, to think of "subject" as a vision of a character or mood or action which presents itself and is grasped by the author—sometimes in a sudden creative image, sometimes gradually—around which he weaves a story. For the purposes of this study we will define "subject" as the central idea or "truth" that determines the characteristics of the story.

Most critics apparently assume that the notion of subject or idea is subsumed in the term, "story," and they begin with story as the determinant of form in the novel. This view is typified by Barbara Hardy's statement: "If the novel does not possess the form of a story then it is not a novel."[9] Forster's oft-quoted comment reiterates: ". . . the novel tells a story. That is the fundamental aspect without which it could not exist. That is the highest factor common to all novels."[10] To distinguish "story" from "subject" here, we shall think of "story" as simply what happens next. It is a narrative of events in a temporal sequence.[11] "Story" is the action of a novel.

Plot is a more complex concept than story because it involves a logic of causality as well as of time. According to Aristotle in his discussion of poetic wholes, plot is the most inclusive and architectonic of the four structural elements which he places in descending order of importance as: plot, character, thought and diction. Richard Crane has studied the Aristotelian divisions and adapted them in his own conception of "plot" as a synthesis of action, character and thought. Action can be understood as story; character, of course, as the persons about whom the story is written, their relationships to each other and to their circumstances; and thought, as the motivation and attraction of characters, which involves a moral dimension.

They are distinct parts in the sense of being variable factors in the complex problem of composing works which, when completed, will produce their effects, synthetically, as organic wholes. . . .[12]
It is impossible, therefore, to state adequately what any plot is unless we include in our formula all three of the elements or causes of which the plot is a synthesis; and it follows also that plots will differ in structure accordingly as one or another of the three causal ingredients is employed as the synthesizing principle. There are, thus, plots of action, plots of character and plots of thought.[13]

Accepting Crane's statements as a full explication of "plot," we can see that as a term it is intimately related to the structure of a novel.

The concept of structure is the most elusive of critical principles to be dealt with in this study, because it depends upon the organic life of the novel with reference only to the interrelation of its parts.[14] The form in a novel is likely to be irregular and highly individual so that the effectiveness of the whole lies not in its correspondence to any external criteria but in its artistic integration. As Tolstoy put it, "This indeed is one of the significant facts about a true work of art—that its content in its entirety can be expressed only by itself."[15] Even the terms *unity, coherence* and *emphasis*, traditionally used to evaluate pattern within smaller units of writing, attempt to define "structure" indirectly.

Unity or singleness of vision is assumed to be essential by most critics who otherwise call it "tone," "perspective," or "worldview." Norman Friedman's description of structure lends an understanding of what is meant here by "unity":

. . . the product of a guiding intelligence which is implicit in the narrative and which shapes the material so as to arouse the reader's expectations with regard to the probable course of events, to cross those expectations with an equally probable contrary course, and then to allay these expectations so that the resultant outcome seems the necessary one.[16]

Coherence or relevance is a topic of much greater critical debate, centering on the disagreement between Jamesians and others as to what materials ought to be included in a novel. On the one hand, Henry James and his followers insist that the structure is analogous to a living organism, an inviolable principle in which each of the parts contains something of the other parts. Anything which does not contribute integrally to the pattern of the book must be lopped away, or, in Forster's words: "Every action or word ought to count; it ought to be economical and spare; even when complicated it should be organic and free from dead matter."[17] On the other hand, critics such as Barbara Hardy attack the Jamesians for going too far in their demands for tightening what can sometimes validly be a loose structure. They defend the inclusion of apparently irrelevant or loosely relevant materials which coarsen the texture and roughen the edges of the novel.[18] The debate would seem to concern critical taste more than principle, since both sides agree that the novel grows out of the moral and metaphysical views of its author.

Unity and coherence, then, supply the outline of pattern; emphasis or proportion provides the contours, the points of interest to which the eye is drawn (and which also form the main supports for the narrative). This emphasis may be upon one or several elements in a novel, growing always from the central meaning. Emphasis was less a criteria of early novelists, whose panoramic or epic qualities far outweighed their finer aesthetic sense, than it was in the later development of modern fiction.

Therefore, beyond the consensus that somehow a novel "ought to hang together," Western critics offer little help in getting at the specifics of pattern (or structure). Perhaps the elusiveness of the term, novel, derives from the sprawling nature of the genre, which seems capable of encompassing and digesting new and related story forms as they are created. As Northrop Frye points out, the problem is partly a matter of semantics: lacking a word for a work of prose fiction, we make do with "novel" for everything, thereby losing its only real meaning as the name of a genre.[19]

Indeed, a thoroughly acceptable definition of the term

[20]

"novel" is not easy to find. Forster's description of it as "any fictitious prose work over 50,000 words" does not touch on form at all. *Webster's New International Dictionary of the English Language,* Second Edition, gives a more complete definition:

A fictitious prose tale of considerable length in which characters and actions professing to represent those of real life are portrayed in a plot. . . . Novels usually deal with the passions, *esp.* love.

At least two ideas need further amplification and refinement, which the critics afford. The first is the fact of the novel depicting human experience, resounding in Forster's affirmation: "The intensely stifling human quality of the novel is not to be avoided; the novel is sogged with humanity."[20] The second is a question of technique: how does one portray "real life"?

The critics answer:

. . . [through concreteness based on] the premise, or primary convention, that the novel is a full and authentic report of human experience, and is therefore under an obligation to satisfy its reader with such details of the story as the individuality of their actions, details which are presented through a more largely referential use of language than is common in other literary forms.[21]

Another perspective may be gained by comparing the novel with other literary genres. Dorothy Van Ghent, for example, explains that while the novel uses many discursive methods unavailable to the drama, it also draws heavily on the dramatic method, ". . . for it represents human beings *as if* in tangible space and time, that is 'scenically' placed and related." "The procedure of the novel," she continues, "is to individualize."[22]

There is a great deal of critical discussion as to what

extent the novelist should strive for the particular, or conversely, for an archetypal of universal model; or how one achieves the proper balance between the two. Individual realism in characters begins in the eighteenth century with the philosophical thought of Descartes and Locke, who took the position that truth can be perceived by the individual through his senses. As Ian Watt explains, the plot was most immediately affected; novelists began to reject the traditional plots culled from mythology, history, legend and earlier literature, and instead to develop their own plots, based on empirical experience. This change led to the particularization of character and setting:

the plot had to be acted out by particular people in particular circumstances, rather than, as had been common in the past, by general human types against a background primarily determined by the appropriate literary convention.

This literary change was analogous to the rejection of universals and the emphasis on particulars which characterises philosophic realism.[23]

Yet some vestige of the universal remains essential, since the persons in a novel represent humanity and must therefore possess qualities identifiable with the human condition; and there seems to be agreement that a fusion of the typical and peculiar is necessary to the creation of a great character, while relative proportions between the general and specific vary with the literary period. Overall, the individualization of character is one of the chief elements of the novel. Despite the emphasis on realistic detail, however, characters cannot simply be taken from life and transplanted into the novel, ". . . real people are too complex and too disorganized for books. They aren't simple enough."[24]

This reciprocal relationship between the characters

and the story in a novel raises the question of how many qualities may be dictated by the total moral or symbolic pattern of the novel before the "felt life" of the character becomes unnatural—again, a source of contention between Jamesians and non-Jamesians. The former, Robert Louis Stevenson in perfect accord, feel that pattern can hardly go too far.[25] The non-Jamesians object to the sacrifice of individuality of character to the need for relevance above all else, which consequently saps the vitality of characters and makes them go "dry and thin."[26] Any judgment concerning the realism of character, then, is intimately connected with an evaluation of his place in the formal structure of the novel—if that structure has distorted his verisimilitude or if he has been allowed to develop organically within and from it.

A character's establishment in a human situation and organic connection with it requires him to act upon it and be acted upon in some way consonant with the personality traits with which he has been endowed by the author. The drawing of a character, Crane contends, creates expectations in the reader which involve him emotionally in the moral and ethical life of the character and in how the problems faced by the character are going to be solved.[27] This unfolding of character presupposes a human depth out of which qualities can be pulled, or a fullness of dimension can be uncovered. It is obvious that secondary characters, having no life outside of their function in the novel, generally do not lend themselves to this kind of process.

We must finally distinguish between major and minor characters. Unfortunately this distinction involves the same disagreement between Jamesians and non-Jamesians centered on the subordination of character to story. Elizabeth Bowen suggests an analysis and separation of important characters from less important ones on the basis of the number of alternatives open to them: "The novelist must allot (to the point of rationing) psychological space. The 'hero', 'heroine' and 'villain' (if any) are, by agreement, allowed most range."[28] Barbara Hardy, reacting against such a division of characters, suggests fluid categories in which major characters play functional roles in given circumstances, and functional characters at times are raised vividly into major roles.[29] Miss Hardy's concept grows out of her idea of a much more tenuous link between incidents in the novel than James would accept.

With these definitions and distinctions in mind, we can proceed to an analysis of *The Dream of the Red Chamber* to determine by which criteria it satisfies the requirements for a novel, to isolate the techniques which create each of the integral parts, and finally to seize on the larger patterns and structure of the book, its unique design and moral imperative.

(2)

Narrative Style

THE OPENING chapter of *The Dream of the Red Chamber*
recounts a most curious myth, which seems dis-
sociated from the main narrative that unfolds in
chronological time, but which actually previews the
novel, like a dumb show before a play,[1] touching on all
the significant themes and lines of action. Here the author establishes the standard of reality by which the
Chias are to be judged: the Taoist standard of non-artificiality, opposing nature to man, glorifying spontaneity.
By the Great Mythical Mountain under the Nonesuch
Bluff the pre-incarnation history of the Immortal Stone
Page (Pao-yü) and the Crimson Flower (Tai-yü)[2] is revealed, explaining the reason for their descent into the
Red Dust, or mortal world. Overhearing a Buddhist
monk and Taoist priest describing the Red Dust, the
Stone addresses this uncommon pair, who in turn warn
him of the vanity of earthly life:

It is true that the Red Dust has its joys, . . . but they are
evanescent and illusory. Moreover, there every happiness is
spoiled by a certain lack, and all good things are poisoned by
the envy and covetousness of other men, so that in the end you
will find the pleasure outweighed by sorrow and sadness.

(Wang, p. 2)

But the Stone is already "involved in a romance that
must be enacted on earth" (Wang, p. 8) and desires to
visit the Red Dust. Accordingly, he is transformed into

[25]

a precious jade and uniquely engraved through the supernatural powers of the monk and priest, who decide to
accompany him on his journey and to observe and guide
his actions. In effect, it is they who record the chronicle
of the Stone, and, however lightly they are treated in this
pseudo-literary role, it is their commentary that gives
initial form to the story. The Crimson Flower, in a
dilemma as to how she can repay the Stone for his kind
attentions, vows to repay him with tears if the two of
them are sent to the Red Dust. Hearing her resolution
the Taoist exclaims,

I never heard of such a thing as repaying a debt with tears. I
imagine the stories of these creatures will be different from the
usual "breeze and moonlight" school.

(Wang, p. 9)

From his words it is clear that theirs will be no common
"romance," but a story of tragic love. Furthermore, it is
through the monk and priest, rather than through any
omniscience of the author, that events are judged in
moral terms. Throughout the novel they periodically
reappear to "set things right."

At the outset then, the characters must cross the
boundary between Heaven and the Great Void Illusion
Land (earth) through a stone archway supported on pillars inscribed:

When the unreal is taken for the real, then the real
becomes unreal;
Where non-existence is taken for existence, then existence
becomes non-existence.

(Wang, p. 11)

This couplet underlines the central duality of appearance and reality in the novel; it implies that earthly existence is but part of a greater life, the life incarnated in

[26]

the Buddhist of Infinite Space and the Taoist of Bound-
less Time. Essentially, all the characters, but Pao-yü and
Tai-yü in particular, are taking part in "the little drama
of the Red Dust" (Wang, p. 9) only temporarily, before
they resume their lives in some other place or form. The
physicality of the boundary, the great stone arch—indeed, the highly specific geography of Heaven, with its
identifiable landmarks (Green Meadows Peak, the Palace
of Vermilion Clouds, etc.) and concrete existence in time
and space—reinforces this sense of the continuity of life.
Heaven becomes the "real" world of non-being, while
earth is the artificial world, a temporary place.

Once through the arch, the monk and priest realize
they have forgotten to register the Stone in Heaven and
they turn back to do so. Their conversation is overheard
in a dream by Chen Shih-yin, a man from a well-to-do
and respected Soochow family, who cares nothing for
fame or fortune. He is fond of wine, which upon awakening he pours generously for himself and a guest, a
young scholar intent on taking the Metropolitan Examinations. In a near-drunken state, Shih-yin offers to pay
the aspirant's way to the Capital. That same day, failing
to heed the warning of the "mangy monk" and the priest,
who have wandered by and asked him to give them his
daughter, Lotus, as a sacrifice to Buddha, Shih-yin subsequently loses the child; she is kidnapped when the nurse
momentarily leaves her alone at a fireworks display.
Thereafter the grief-stricken Shih-yin is beset with a
sudden series of misfortunes which he is powerless to
control: his house burns to the ground, his farmlands are
ravaged by floods, then by bandits and troops. Finally he
throws himself on the mercy of his cunning father-in-
law, who manages to extract from Shih-yin the last of his
money and then accuses his son-in-law of laziness. While
walking in the street one day, Shih-yin hears a Taoist

singing the song of "Forget and be free." Shih-yin intuitively understands the meaning, and he himself elaborates on the theme of the transcience of earthly things:

> Boast not that you wear powder and rouge well,
> But grieve that your temples will soon be covered with frost.
> Tonight a pair of cooing doves under red bridal curtains,
> Tomorrow a heap of bleached bones like those of yesteryear.

> •   •   •

> What bustle and confusion, as one set of actors exits and another enters,
> Each taking the illusory for the real.
> What stupidity; for in the end, in the end
> One only wears out one's fingers for someone else's trousseau.

> (Wang, p. 18)

Again the reader is struck by the vivid imagery of aging and death, the comparison of mortal life with a stage play, which ends all too quickly for the actors, whose cosmetics and fine clothes cannot stay the effects of time. The moral implicit in these lines is not at all what the Western reader, familiar with the adage "Eat, drink and be merry . . . ," might deduce. But to the Chinese reader versed in Taoist thought the implication is clear. Taoism is based on the belief that nature is supreme and man must do nothing to violate the natural order, or *tao*, which attains its human embodiment in the mystic ascetic and its logical end in the doctrine of non-action: "do nothing, desire nothing, for the only true reality lies in harmony with the *tao*, and the only true action is non-action." By this standard the narrative dwells on actions and descriptions which are mere appearances. Once this standard is established the reader is rarely reminded again that they are, indeed, appearances; except, as we have said, where the Buddhist monk or Taoist priest exert their supernatural powers to set wrongs right, or where one of the characters becomes a monk, priest, or nun, renouncing the "real," that is mortal (hence artificial) world to enter the true world of non-being and non-action. This is the choice Shih-yin has made. It is therefore not surprising when the reader learns immediately afterwards that Shih-yin disappears from his household forever, leaving his wife to wonder about his fate and to support herself by sewing.

The disappearance of Shih-yin provides the tenuous link through which the Chia family is introduced. Chia Yü-ts'un, the poor scholar upon whom Shih-yin once bestowed a gift of silver, has that very day been installed as prefect of Yingtienfu, and he has sent a servant to seek his friend Shih-yin at the home of his father-in-law, in order that as prefect Yü-ts'un might express his gratitude and return favors to his former benefactor. The reader learns through the ensuing exposition that prior to his appointment as prefect Yü-ts'un was tutor to the only child of the salt commissioner in Yangchow, a daughter named Tai-yü. Following the death of the commissioner's wife after a prolonged illness, Tai-yü has been invited to live with her maternal relatives, the Chias, in the Capital. In idle gossip with his friend Yü-ts'un, a curio shop owner alludes to the Chia family in the riddle of the centipede that dies but never falls down. Subsequently Yü-ts'un conducts his pupil to the Capital, where he calls on Chia Cheng, through whose influence Yü-ts'un obtained the office of prefect.

Even when we meet them, the family is not what it was, nor the members what they appear to be to Tai-yü, whose arrival follows a brief discourse on the genealogy and personalities of the two branches of the family that occupy the *Yungkuofu* and the *Ningkuofu.** Having heard much talk about the wealth and elegance of her relatives, Tai-yü is predisposed to remark on the trappings of luxury she sees everywhere about her: the number of servants and their costumes, the imposing entrances to the mansions, and the painted and carved interior of the Yungkuofu with its flowered verandas and caged birds. Tai-yü's arrival approaches a ceremonial, beginning with her being carried into the city in a sedan chair, in a kind of procession. In her honor the Matriarch has declared a holiday from school for the young cousins and ordered tea to be served. Her aunts, as they introduce themselves to her, enhance this aura of spectacle. They are all beautifully adorned and elegant in their manners, especially her aunt Wang Hsi-fêng, who rushes in late with a loud laugh. Tai-yü is impressed with the young woman's air of self-assurance and the large amount of jewelry she wears, and, too, with her conscious efforts to make the newcomer feel at home. Still, Tai-yü senses a hardness in her gaily clad aunt, who begs Tai-yü to call on her if she wants anything. Throughout the day Tai-yü guards her every step and word so as not to make a social blunder. Her aunts are delighted with her behavior and question her in detail about her mother's death and her own peculiar illness, for which she takes gingseng pills.

At length Tai-yü is conducted to the eastern wing of the mansion, where she is to meet Chia Shê and Chia Cheng; but both men are indisposed and her introduc-

*Literally "Family Residence of the Duke of Yungkuo" and "Family Residence of the Duke of Ningkuo," which were honorary titles conferred by the Emperor in times past. Yungkuo Kung means "Duke of the Honor of the Throne"; Ningkuo Kung, "Duke of the Peace of the Throne." The Yungkuofu is elsewhere called the Western Mansion or western wing, and the Ningkuofu called the Eastern Mansion or eastern wing.

tion to each is put off. At this point Wang Fu-jen tells Tai-yü about her son, Pao-yü, warning her that she must not pay the least attention to his wild behavior nor take anything he says seriously. Just as the women of the family are seated for dinner, each member in her proper place, Pao-yü enters. His appearance immediately captivates Tai-yü. She is struck with his charm and beauty and graciousness. As for Pao-yü, there is something in their meeting which evokes both his admiration for Tai-yü, whose features remind him of a delicate flower, and the feeling that he has met this *mei-mei* ("little sister" or "cousin") before. The reader is referred to the episode of the Immortal Stone Page—a tangible connection being made in Pao-yü's inscribed jade pendant that he wears dangling from a silk cord around his neck—and the Crimson Flower of the opening chapter. The suggestion of a relationship between Pao-yü and Tai-yü is reinforced at once by the fact that each is singled out by the Matriarch as a favorite upon whom she lavishes excessive love and attention; and further by Tai-yü's being assigned rooms adjoining those of Pao-yü in the Matriarch's apartment. Pao-yü is also given a hand-maiden, Hsi-jên, who befriends Tai-yü.

The very next day more relatives, the Hsüehs, arrive at the Yungkuofu and are invited to stay. Hsüeh Yi-ma, a sister of Wang Fu-jen, takes up residence with her son, Hsüeh P'an, who has come to the Capital seeking pleasure, and her daughter, Pao-ch'ai, who is a girl of great poise and wisdom. Tai-yü senses the entrance of this other girl cousin as an intrusion. She is jealous of Pao-ch'ai, who, in comparison with her own haughty and aloof manner, seems even-tempered and without affectations. Pao-yü, however, is unaware of any change in the situation.

It was said that on his first birthday, Pao-yü chose,

from among the numerous toys and objects strewn within his reach, powder and rouge and hair ornaments. His father took this as a sign that the boy would grow up to be dissolute and lascivious. Ever since, Pao-yü has shown a more than ordinary sensitivity to feminine things and preferred the company of girls to that of boys, once defending his choice with the strange explanation "that girls are made of water while men are made of clay and that is why he feels purified and invigorated in the presence of the one and contaminated and oppressed within the presence of another" (Wang, p. 26). Before the advent of these two cousins into his life, Pao-yü's interest in girls, though intense, is a fairly general one. It apparently makes little difference whom he is with, as long as he has female companionship. Once they are present, however, Pao-yü focuses his attention on Tai-yü and Pao-ch'ai, seeking their company in particular. His earliest attentions are balanced, and by virtue of his simple nature, he feels equally happy with both or either of them. This tendency offends Tai-yü and elicits from Pao-yü several times a tender apology.

Connecting the introductory material with the main action of the novel is a dream interlude in which the past, present, and future of "the Twelve Maidens of Chin-ling" is foretold in cryptic verse to Pao-yü. These maidens represent the twelve young women of Pao-yü's generation, including his cousins and serving maids. The dream takes place in the chamber of Ch'in K'e-ch'ing.[3] After his dinner Pao-yü is sleepy and wants to nap, but he dislikes the elaborately decorated room in the main apartments to which he is led. K'e-ch'ing then invites Pao-yü to use her own fragrant room, which she claims is "fit for immortals" (Wang, p. 52).

Like the myth of the first chapter, the dream unfolds on a subconsious and/or pre-existential level, involving a re-crossing through the great stone arch into the "Sea of Passion and Heaven of Love" (Wang, p. 54). The dream contains identical phrases and names from the earlier chapter, notably the couplet inscribed on the pillars about existence and non-existence, with the additional lines:

> Enduring as heaven and earth—no love however ancient can ever die;
> Timeless as light and shadow—no debt of breeze and moonlight can ever be repaid.
>
> (Wang, p. 54)

If the earlier scene may be construed as a birth myth, then the dream sequence is a passage from childhood into adolescence, in which the mysteries of love and human sexuality are revealed to Pao-yü, who is confused by the verses and claims not to understand. It is therefore fitting that the speaker in the dream is the Goddess of Disillusionment and her only praise of Pao-yü, the pronouncement that he is "the most licentious of men" (Wang, p. 58). His excesses, she suggests, are of a most subtle nature, likely to make him appear strange to the rest of the world, although he will always be welcome in the ladies' quarters. Her words somehow echo Chia Cheng's statements upon discovering his child's choice of rouge and powder.

The dream enhances the idea, associated with every mention of Pao-yü, that he belongs to a special breed of men. Following feasting and singing, reminiscent of a primitive rite for a prince, Pao-yü is introduced to the "play of rain and clouds." The Goddess takes great pains to distinguish between this lustful act and real love which he must learn by studying Confucius and Mencius. Pao-yü then disports himself with the bride in his dream; later he is attacked by monsters. He awakens

[33]

terrified, jolting K'e-ch'ing by calling out her secret childhood name.

Hsi-jên, who answers his outcry along with three other maids, soon discovers that her master has had a "wet dream," and he tells her everything. Eventually she gives in to his coaxing, realizing that she will someday be his mistress, and they re-enact the "play of rain and clouds" together. This only increases the tender devotion Hsi-jên already feels toward her master. He, in turn, treats her even more kindly.

Essentially, Pao-yü's knowledge seems to age the boy, thrusting upon him a necessary responsibility for his own actions. This idea is supported by the fact that in the joint family system, a liaison like that between Pao-yü and Hsi-jên, if known, might be sanctioned. In Chinese society the secondary wife, or concubine, and the children she bears may be considered members of the family and have a recognized place in the household, although, of course, they are without claim to lands or title. Pao-yü, in fact, has a half-brother, Chia Huan, a boy of unpredictable disposition, who is the son of Pao-yü's father, Chia Cheng, and the concubine Chao Yi-niang.

The main action of the novel proceeds from the middle of Chapter 6, with the visit of Liu *Lao-lao*.[4] Again the arrival of a distant relative ends in a family reunion, but both the occasion and the reception of *Lao-lao's* visit are different from those with which the reader is already familiar, those of Tai-yü and the Hsüehs. *Lao-lao* is related indirectly, that is, through a petty official in the Capital who had admired the prestige and wealth of the Chias and years back "joined family" with the grandfather of Wang Hsi-fêng. That branch of the family is now poverty-stricken, and *Lao-lao* is the only one of her kin who is not too proud to approach her rich relatives for money. Plainly she is a country cousin, lacking the manners and polished speech prized by the Chias, or, rather, choosing to play the country bumpkin to amuse the company and thereby gain her goal. Her visit throws into relief the false values of the Chias. The disregard with which she is generally treated, even by the servants, and the mockery made of her at the dinner table, stand in marked contrast to her own good humor.

At the same time, there are at least two similarities between the visits of Liu *Lao-lao* and Tai-yü that are important to note. The first is the impression that the scent, furnishings, and dress make on the visitors to the mansion. Tai-yü is enchanted. Liu *Lao-lao* is awed to the point where she mistakes a maid for Hsi-fêng; then, when she is finally face-to-face with the young mistress, she is almost too embarrassed to ask for money and needs prompting from the steward's wife before she will voice her request. The second is the similar role Hsi-fêng plays in setting each of the visitors at ease. In the case of Tai-yü this is accomplished by the mere suggestion of her authority, with Hsi-fêng's instruction that the girl must report to her any inattention or abuse on the part of the servants. Her position as second in the household, next to the Matriarch, is firmly established by the time of Liu *Lao-lao's* arrival, and the country aunt comments on the unusualness of this situation: "I imagine our . . . [Hsi-fêng] cannot be more than twenty at the most. . . . It is remarkable that she should be put in charge of things when she is still so young."

Hsi-fêng attempts to demonstrate her capability by giving *Lao-lao* twenty ounces of silver. This transaction is doubly ironical, first because an amount which Hsi-fêng deems insignificant seems a fortune to *Lao-lao*. Her astonishment at receiving such a sum in cash is further set against the disdain of the steward's wife for the small piece of silver offered her by *Lao-lao* as a tip. The payment also exposes Hsi-fêng's duplicity. She gives away money entrusted to her by the Matriarch to buy new clothes for the maids—money which is therefore not hers to bestow—to a woman whom she does not think of as a *real* relative, and she insists all the while that the family, despite their prosperity, has trouble making ends meet. Surely Hsi-fêng's motivation, an overweening vanity that requires that she make a grand gesture to enhance her position in the eyes of the poor woman, is as curious as the homily *Lao-lao* utters sympathetically: "A camel that dies of starvation is larger than a fat horse."

From their first mention, then, the Chias are shown in a stage of decay. They preserve the appearance of prosperity, but the family fortunes are in fact said to be declining as a result of mismanagement[5] and the bloodline deteriorating. These facts are hinted at in conversation between minor characters, then substantiated in the introductory family scenes. Just before the entrance of *Lao-lao* the narrator[6] expresses consternation at how to begin handling such a large amount of materials and indicates a somewhat circumstantial and random starting point:

Although the Yungkuofu was not unduly large, there were over three hundred mouths, from master to servant and mistress to maid. Although the household duties were not unduly burdensome, there occurred daily at least scores of things to be attended to. For one who attempts to unravel the story, the problems are as perplexing as a mass of hemp with a thousand loose ends. Just at the point when we were at a loss as to what to use for the further development of our story, there came to the Yungkuofu a visitor from a poor family only remotely related to the Chias. . . .

(Wang, p. 61)

[36]

The structure of the novel is implicit in this statement.

The subject is the Chia family; or more specifically, it is in the complexity of the everyday lives of its individual members that the theme of appearance and reality is explored in minute detail as it relates to the downfall of the Chias from their position of apparent wealth and prestige. Therefore, in the first few chapters a great deal of care is given to describing the natures of individual characters and their relationships, as well as the physical setting—the two mansions and their grounds—where most of the significant action takes place.*

The action is mainly episodic, following a direct and chronological line. In general, the episodes in the earlier portions of the book continue to describe the tenor of life in the mansions; show through ordinary incidents the day-by-day rhythm of existence; illustrate in accounts of family gatherings, illnesses or quarrels, the weaknesses and strengths of the noble family; depict the personalities, attitudes, expectations, and fears of the characters; and build a picture of an apparently strong house set atop shaky foundations. The episodes in the latter portion of the book focus more directly on the recurrent misfortunes which bring the household near destruction. In the final chapter there is a brief upward movement in the story, showing the process of rebuilding.

Each of the episodes is linked to the next by a repetitive device which is a carry-over from the oral tradition behind the novel. The last words of a chapter in a traditional Chinese novel are always an invitation to read the next chapter to find out what is happening and why.[7] The particular phrase at the end of Chapter 5, which

---

*Representational art work based on the scenery and characters of the *Dream of the Red Chamber* has been popular since the novel was first published, and the Hong Kong edition contains a detailed drawing of the *Ta-kuan-yüan* Garden, with its pavilions, groves and bridges clearly identified.

refers to Pao-yü's calling out the childhood name of Ch'in K'e-ch'ing in his sleep, is: "If you don't know why this was, the next chapter will explain." The connection is made in Chapter 6 when Pao-yü and his personal maid re-enact the marital consummation of his dream. Few of these invitatory phrases remain in the translations, so that an entire episode is completed within a single chapter in the English versions; but in the original there is this kind of interlocking, which reinforces the temporal and causal relationships between events.

Thus the supernatural Taoist priest and Buddhist monk introduced in Chapter 1, who stand outside of time, take their place and perform within the chronological framework of the narrative, without disturbing the essential forward movement of the plot. The dream sequences, too, fit specifically into the time-space of the novel. As we have seen, careful attention is given to physical and geographical details of setting, and to a logical unfolding of the various story lines, both of which contain a curious blending of the supernatural and everyday.

Occasionally this forward movement is arrested to detail the background of a new character or to clarify some event with a previous history, such as Liu *Lao-lao's* mission at Yungkuofu. At other times the narrative expands laterally; that is, one episode is finished and the actions of a different set of characters, simultaneous to the first, are described, often with dramatic effect. This we see illustrated, for example, during the period of general excitement devoted to planning and building the "Grand View Garden," the *Ta-kuan-yüan*, in preparation for the visit of the Chia's eldest daughter, now the Imperial Concubine, who by law must have a suitable place in which to be received. The preparations occupy the time and thoughts of all the older family members and a large staff of underlings, running to much work and great expense. The original text sets forth the details of the preparations minutely, but they occupy little space in the Kuhn translation and still less in the Wang. Subsequent to the description of these preparations, the reader learns of the death of Pao-yü's nephew and schoolmate, which occurred while the grounds were being made ready and caused Pao-yü such grief that he was distracted and unable to enjoy the freedom from supervision made possible by his father's involvement in the preparations. The comment about the death and its effect on Pao-yü are made in passing, as if in examining a magnificent *objet d'art* some tiny flaw was found to ruin the perfect beauty of the thing; and the whole reception becomes somehow ludicrous and wasteful.

Besides their unfolding in a temporal sequence, the events in *The Dream of the Red Chamber* relate causally one to another, and each to the central subject. The plot is highly manipulated by the close social relationships among the characters, both those imposed by the intimacy of communal living and the network of familial obligations rooted in Confucian tradition, and those growing spontaneously from personal feeling. An individual's interest in the book depends on how he comes to terms with those social, ethical and moral demands, and how individual reactions influence the resolves of others in a continuing vibration.

The subject of the Chia decline is pursued in two distinct stories or lines of action. One story focuses on Pao-yü and his two cousins, Tai-yü and Pao-ch'ai. Their relationships shift subtly as Pao-yü awakens to the variety of female beauty, then violently break apart when his choice of a bride is thwarted and he is tricked into a hasty arranged marriage with Pao-ch'ai while Tai-yü languishes on her deathbed. These developing relationships

[39]

affect not only the three most immediately involved, but all those whose lives touch on theirs, insofar as the cousins represent the youngest generation of Chias, who will one day inherit the family fortunes and offices.

Pao-yü is drawn to Tai-yü initially by a sense of an experience shared in the remote past. He is repeatedly sensitive and compassionate toward her, submerging his own terrible temper, evident in the scene of their first meeting when he rips his jade pendant from his neck and throws it on the floor. Whenever there is conflict between them—and Tai-yü's uncontrollable jealousy flares into many rages—it is Pao-yü who apologizes. He accepts the blame and exhibits a remarkable degree of patience and understanding, always coaxing Tai-yü back into a good mood—as, for example, in the scene where Tai-yü destroys a lotus-leaf purse she is making as a present for Pao-yü because she thinks he has given away the purse she previously made for him. Pao-yü has just opened his robe to reveal the original purse tucked safely in his belt when she snatches it from him and begins to cut it up:

> "Dear *Mei mei*, give it back to me!"
> "First say 'please' nicely!"
> "Please, please! And you will give me the perfume bag you promised me too, won't you?"
> "That will depend entirely on my mood."
>
> (Kuhn, p. 134)

The scene ends with "peace . . . restored between the two lovers, who seemed destined for such endless quarrels and complaints" (Wang, p. 142).

In effect the love story of Tai-yü and Pao-yü is told through a series of lovers' quarrels: Tai-yü's anger at finding Pao-yü visiting the ailing Pao-ch'ai, Tai-yü's refusal to accept Pao-yü's gift of a prayer bracelet on her return from Soochow because it has been worn before, Tai-yü's pointed remarks about the similarity between Pao-yü's jade pendant and Pao-ch'ai's gold locket, Tai-yü's humiliation when a resemblance is suggested between herself and an actress who performs at the Yung-kuofu. In each case Tai-yü's outbursts are encouraged by Pao-yü's solicitousness, inviting her to further scenes that elicit tender words of forgiveness and declarations of undying love.

This pattern engenders a strong expectation that Tai-yü will eventually be Pao-yü's bride. The cousins appear to share like temperaments and interests. Both have a tendency to melancholia and morbid thoughts, deriving from their mutual sensitivity and the fact that death has taken away someone close to each of them. Both enjoy natural beauty and literary works, and find great amusement in reading frivolous novels and improvising occasional poetry. And both are coddled, self-centered children, used to lives of luxury and given to tantrums when their desires are frustrated. As the intimacy between Tai-yü and Pao-yü develops, the reader judges with increasing certainty that such a marriage will be beset with difficulties, based on the evidence of their frequent arguments, and the realization that their common traits are in fact the weaknesses in both of their characters, added to the ever-present sense of Tai-yü's unlucky destiny.

The reader is at the same time aware of Pao-ch'ai's role, symbolized by her gold locket, which is inscribed with a couplet similar to that on Pao-yü's jade and is considered to be a sign of their common fate. Pao-yü's pendant is engraved:

Never Lose   Never Forget
Immortal Life Everlasting. . . .

and Pao-ch'ai's:

> Never Relinquish, Never Abandon
> Long Life, Forever Enduring.*
>
> (Wang, p. 81)

The fact that they form a perfect four-line stanza and that also an old mangy-headed monk, reminiscent of the guardian of Pao-yü's stone, gave her the lines and advised her to have them engraved on a medallion, strongly suggests a union between Pao-yü and Pao-ch'ai.

The tendency is for the relationships to polarize and the reader's sympathies to waver. At one extreme, the love between Pao-yü and Tai-yü fulfills the reader's expectations of the typical romance, in that the lovers are completely self-indulgent, expressing their feelings freely and withdrawing together to hoard their mutual love. At the other extreme, the union between Pao-yü and Pao-ch'ai is favored by social considerations—Pao-ch'ai's abilities are those best suited for the future mistress of the Yungkuofu—and by supernatural signs. Thus the reader suspects Pao-ch'ai is the "right" bride.

The relationships among the three cousins are by no means static. As we have seen, Pao-yü unwittingly provokes Tai-yü's jealousy by his attentions to Pao-ch'ai, and Tai-yü grows even more sardonic as it seems the powers of the gold bracelet will cross her own expectations of marriage. Pao-ch'ai reacts to these outbursts with characteristic patience and good sense. Generally

*In the Kuhn translation (p. 59): Never lose me, never forget me!
Glorious life—lasting prosperity!

· · ·

Never leave me, never reject me!
Precious youth—lasting bloom!

her response is one of silence. For example, when she remembers that their cousin Shih Hsiang-yün also wears a little gold unicorn like the one Pao-yü has singled out and kept from a number of gifts given him by monks at the temple, Pao-ch'ai is praised by T'an-ch'un for her good memory:

"Her observation and memory are limited in most things," Tai-yü said, scornfully, "but when it comes to jewelry worn by some people she is all-observant."
This was an allusion to the gold-and-jade destiny, but no one saw the real significance of her remark, and Pao-ch'ai pretended not to have heard.

(Wang, p. 224)

Known as a woman of solid character, Pao-ch'ai is depended upon as a quiet peace-maker. She is called upon, for example, to manage her brother's shrewish wife and to help in running the mansion when Hsi-fêng is sick. By virtue of her maturity she becomes the family's choice of a bride for Pao-yü. Tai-yü, on the other hand, strains her relationships with other members of the family through her fits of jealousy and temper, and consequently is rejected as Pao-yü's bride, leading to her eventual death. Pao-yü, always tender and compassionate, tries to please both of his cousins and offend no one. He allows his love for Tai-yü to envelop him so totally, however, that he cannot accept the reality of his marriage to Pao-ch'ai; he lives in a constant state of tension vacillating between despair and resentment of his new wife. Pao-ch'ai, however, remains firm in her affection.

The immediate family and servants are all involved in the story, especially at the crucial moment of the marriage. Pao-yü's personal waiting maid, Hsi-jên, fears Tai-yü's high strung, petulant nature, but also understands

[43]

the force of Pao-yü's love* and the effect its denial will have on him morally and physically. Despite her own preference for Pao-ch'ai, who would be a gentler wife and a kinder mistress, Hsi-jên pleads with his mother and grandmother to settle on a marriage between Pao-yü and Tai-yü. The Matriarch has other ideas. Feeling that Pao-yü's mental inconstancy will be stabilized by marriage and that Pao-ch'ai possesses the requisite qualities for his wife, the old woman urges the immediate marriage of Pao-yü and Pao-ch'ai. Hsi-fêng, foreseeing Pao-yü's probable reaction to such a match, arranges for the wedding to be secret and the bride veiled. The deception works, and Pao-yü believes he is marrying Tai-yü; when he lifts the veil he finds Pao-ch'ai in her stead. The ailing Tai-yü learns of the marriage and soon dies. Pao-yü, grieved and in shock, is unable to perform his duties as a proper husband.

The second main story line centers on Wang Hsi-fêng, whose career becomes a direct instrument of the Chias' decline. The grandniece of the Matriarch, she exploits the authority entrusted to her by the Matriarch to augment her own wealth and status, dispensing money according to her whim and acting as secret intermediary in a series of intrigues to obtain personal favors. Her ultimate exposure brings disgrace on the family. Hsi-fêng's precarious budgeting reduces them all to near bankruptcy, and her jealous plotting contributes to a network of vice and death.

From her entrance into the novel, Wang Hsi-fêng is singled out for her exceptional talent, wit and self-assur-

*Pao-yü's first full declaration of love for Tai-yü is in fact made to Hsi-jên whose presence he has mistaken—his back turned to her in embarrassment at his own words—for that of Tai-yü.

ance. She interjects loud laughter into the staid atmosphere, a sign of the great cracks she will forge in the life of the family. Upon the death of Chia Chen's daughter-in-law, Ch'in K'e-ch'ing, Hsi-fêng is placed in charge of the elaborate funeral ceremonies at the Ningkuofu, a position of great responsibility in such a wealthy, aristocratic family, and one rarely given to so young a person. Just prior to her death, K'e-ch'ing appears to Hsi-fêng in a dream, instructing her that in order to save the family and insure their future Hsi-fêng must buy large tracts of land bordering on the cemetery and use the income to perpetuate ancestral offerings and support the family school.[8] Hsi-fêng does not heed this advice, although she is almost immediately in a position to do so.

As mistress of the Yungkuo mansion, Hsi-fêng controls the servants' payroll. This ready access to sums of money excites her propensity to greed and officiousness, as well as her sense of vanity. We have already examined her behavior with Liu *Lao-lao*. Her dealings with the Abbess of the Convent of the Water Moon, who asks Hsi-fêng to intercede on the part of a friend involved in a lawsuit, is again motivated by pride. Hsi-fêng refuses to act on the Abbess's request until the woman purposely hints that the reason for Hsi-fêng's refusal is that she lacks the power and influence to do something about the case. This argument works, and Hsi-fêng accepts the charge, along with a bribe of three thousand ounces of silver, which she claims she will need to pay emissaries. Actually, the favor is obtained in a single trip. Hsi-fêng keeps most of the silver for herself, saying nothing more about the incident to anyone. This success encourages her to lend sums of money at interest for short terms, between the time the money is given into her keeping and that time when she pays it out. Although these business ventures inconvenience the servants and threaten Hsi-fêng herself with exposure, she has no apparent intention of abandoning the practice.

"The fact is," P'ing-erh whispered, "that the allowance for the month was received from the outside long ago, but Nai-nai [Hsi-fêng] let it out on short-term loans. She expects to collect it in a few days. I wouldn't tell anyone but you, so make sure that you keep it to yourself."

"Why should she want to do that?" Hsi-jên said. "Surely she couldn't be short of funds. One would think her hands were full enough without this additional worry."

"That's what I think too, but that's the way she is. During the last few years she must have made close to a thousand taels a year in interest, what with the money passing through her hands and the money she has been saving out of her own allowance."

(Wang, p. 272)

Her greed has grown beyond her power to control it.

Hsi-fêng's story develops further in her relationship with Chia Jui and her husband, Chia Lien. The former is a cousin whose too-obvious infatuation with Hsi-fêng and attempts to seduce her, reveal a streak of cruelty in her. In addition, her marriage is upset by a fundamental reversal in the traditional roles, since the urbane Chia Lien finds himself "somewhat eclipsed by his wife" (Wang, p. 29). In an attempt to privately right the balance Lien takes to bed with him the more handsome of his pages, then the wanton To Ku-niang, wife of the drunken cook, and finally a concubine, Yu Er-chieh, whom he marries in secret. Hsi-fêng is by nature jealous and possessive, and this trait manifests itself in her relations with her husband. Her constant suspicions provoke frequent scenes between them, drawing out a violent passion that is otherwise disguised under a polished and perfumed facade. Through her maid, whom

[46]

she forces to spy on her husband, Hsi-fêng learns of his secret marriage and torments the concubine, who commits suicide as a result of her humiliation.

It is the many faces that Hsi-fêng wears and her ability to change and adapt them at will, coupled with her central and powerful role in the household, that relate her to the other characters. With the Matriarch she is always attentive and loving; with her husband, always suspicious and on her guard; with the members of the family in a social situation, she is always personable and pleasant, yet in command; with the servants she is always the exacting, capable mistress. Only with her maid, P'ing-erh, does she drop her mask.

Her story touches that of Pao-yü and Pao-ch'ai at numerous points where they act together or because of one another, thereby interweaving the two major stories. Pao-yü, for example, is partially responsible for Hsi-fêng's temporary appointment as mistress of the Ning-kuofu, since it was he who suggested her to his cousin, Chia Chen. Pao-yü and Hsi-fêng are favored by the Matriarch and hated by the concubine Chao Yi-niang, who has them both put under a deathly spell by a wicked, witch-woman to whom she has complained. They are released at the last moment when the mangy monk and lame priest restore the magical powers of Pao-yü's jade, that have been dulled by thirteen years in the Red Dust. And it is Hsi-fêng who is instrumental in keeping secret from Tai-yü and Pao-yü the marriage plans for him and Pao-ch'ai.

These two major story lines, forward-moving and related at various points, are also interwoven with numerous minor stories that contribute to the character development or action and/or reinforce the broader theme of the novel. Some of these stories, like that of Ch'in Chung's love for the nun, Chih Neng, and his friendship with Pao-yü, enter into the main narrative only briefly, then drop out totally. Others, like the escapades of Hsüeh P'an, Pao-ch'ai's brother, enter, drop out, then return again, building up an atmosphere of pervasive corruption through the repetition of an incident or type of behavior. This interweaving of several stories roughens the texture of the novel, giving it the semblance of everyday life. The narrative moves from one small incident to another in a leisurely flow until an episode of some importance arrests the movement, which resumes again slowly.

We can see the casual design of the novel specifically in a brief resume of the action following Liu *Lao-lao*'s visit to the Yungkuofu. The steward's wife, who has witnessed the interview between *Lao-lao* and Hsi-feng, seeks to report it to her mistress, Wang Fu-jen, but finding the latter out, instead visits Pao-ch'ai, who has been ill. Pao-ch'ai details the nature of her chronic illness and the ingredients which make up the "Cold Perfume Pill" prescribed for her by a monk when no other medicine would cure her symptoms. This scene is succeeded by the following sequence of events: the distribution of silk-flower coronets to the twelve young women; Pao-yü's first meeting with Ch'in Chung; the old servant Chiao Ta's drunken invective, which ends with the crude insinuation of adultery between Chia Chen and Ch'in K'e-ch'ing; Pao-yü's and Pao-ch'ai's mutual discovery of the similarity between the inscriptions on each of their pendants; Pao-yü's drinking too much, then— when he returns home—railing against his old childhood nurse because she has eaten the cakes that he was saving as a treat for one of the maids; the Matriarch's granting permission for Ch'in Chung to go to the family school with Pao-yü, and the fracas which ensues after one of the boys accuses Pao-yü, Ch'in Chung and several others of

[48]

improper intimacies; the attempt of the mother of Chin Yung, one of the boys implicated, to use her influence with the Chias to avenge her son, and the abrupt abandoning of her plan, when she herself is threatened with humiliation; and the doctor's diagnosis of Ch'in K'e-ch'ing's illness as grave. The amount of time that elapses is about five days, although there is an undefined period between Ch'in Chung's acceptance as a companion for Pao-yü and their beginning school.

It is obvious that there is a basic unevenness in the importance of each of these scenes to the novel as a whole. Of the scenes outlined, the only one of major significance is the pairing of the jade and gold pendants of Pao-yü and Pao-ch'ai, the symbol of their common destiny, which recurs and contributes to the central, tragic love story. The others vary in importance from those that are relevant only in giving continuity or plausibility to the narrative or in filling out the personalities of the main characters, to those that develop the main story lines. Scenes such as the planned avenging of Chin Yung's disgrace, or Tai-yü's rejection of her flower coronet because it is exactly like the other eleven presented to her cousins, could be eliminated with very little loss to the novel. There are other scenes which are not strictly essential but do add dimension to the personalities and relationships of the immediate family, such as Pao-yü's introduction to Ch'in Chung and their subsequent friendship at school.

The surface nature of the narrative, which keeps the reader at a fixed distance from the characters, makes proportion in the novel difficult to grasp. It is an impersonal account, dependent on alternate passages of description and dialogue, rather than on any of a number of such common narrative devices as memory flashbacks, interjections of the author himself as a persona in the novel, psychological probing into or speculation on the motivations and feelings of a character. The narrative moves back and forth between major and minor characters with apparently equal concern, and the reader must learn to pick out the threads of stories and locate the central characters on the basis of the quantity of evidence presented.

Emphasis in *The Dream of the Red Chamber* is achieved by deliberate repetition. The frequency with which a character is mentioned or appears in scenes closely related to the emerging story lines, and the number and immediacy of human relationships dependent upon him, indicate his importance. Pao-yü, for instance, appears in eight of the twelve scenes just listed. Tai-yü, Pao-ch'ai, Wang Hsi-fêng and Hsi-jên each appear in four. Other characters, such as Wang Fu-jen, the steward's wife, and Chiao Ta, appear only once or twice, and, as in the case of these last two, do not reappear for some time thereafter.

Keeping this general scheme in mind, we can then plot the pattern of the whole novel, which proceeds in the same rambling fashion. The high points in the narrative are, in order: the pre-incarnation story of Pao-yü and Tai-yü (Chapter 1); Pao-yü's first dream (Chapter 5); the death of Ch'in K'e-ch'ing and her appearance to Hsi-fêng, who is shortly thereafter appointed as supervisor of the *Ningkuofu* (Chapter 13); the raising of Yüan-ch'un to the rank of Imperial Concubine, and the building of the *Ta-kuan-yüan* (Chapter 16); the Imperial Concubine's visit (Chapter 18); the spell cast over Pao-yü and Wang Hsi-fêng by a necromancer (Chapter 25); Pao-yü's confession of his love for Tai-yü (Chapter 32); the flogging of Pao-yü by his father (Chapter 33); Wang Hsi-fêng's discovery of her husband with another woman and her ensuing rage (Chapter 44); Yu Erh-chieh's suicide (Chapter 69); the disturbance of an evening party at the *Ning-kuofu* by an eerie sound (Chapter 75); Tai-yü's dream in which Pao-yü cuts out his heart and Pao-yü's awakening with a stabbing pain (Chapters 82–83); the family's agreement on Pao-ch'ai as a bride for Pao-yü (Chapter 84); the begonia's flowering out of season and Pao-yü's loss of the jade (Chapter 94); Pao-yü's marriage and Tai-yü's death (Chapter 97); the appearance of the ghost of Ch'in K'e-ch'ing to Wang Hsi-fêng to reprimand her for not following her instructions to perpetuate ancestral offerings and support the family school on income from purchased burial land (Chapter 101); the arrest of the Matriarch's son, her grand-nephew and his son for intrigue, and the search of the mansion (Chapter 105); the Matriarch's death (Chapter 110); Wang Hsi-fêng's death (Chapter 114); Pao-yü's second dream (Chapter 116); Pao-yü's taking of the Examination and his disappearance (Chapter 119); Pao-yü's appearance to his father on the snow-covered bank of the canal (Chapter 120).

If we look for a pattern in these scenes, we see that it is composed of three major figures: the love triangle, which predominates, becomes increasingly taut, and finally disintegrates under pressure; the expansion and collapse of the power of Hsi-fêng; and the decline and fall of the house of Chia. Surrounding these three figures, which emerge distinctly in such a skeletal outline of the novel, are numerous subordinate scenes and episodes that are either closely relevant, loosely relevant, or irrelevant. The closely relevant scenes fill out the immediate background and further the development of one of these major figures. Such scenes, for instance, as the request for help made by the Abbess of the Water Moon Convent feeds Hsi-fêng's selfish pride, a trait which leads her to disgrace; and the announcement of Tai-yü's maid to Pao-yü that her mistress is leaving causes him to react violently to the disappointing news.

Other less relevant scenes add to the weight of the novel and its somewhat rococo decoration, but contribute only loosely to one of the central figures. The visits of Liu *Lao-lao* provide comic relief, as well as serving to draw a striking contrast between the elaborate social code of the Chia's and the peasants' earthy manner, and tying a loose end of the plot when she saves Hsi-fêng's daughter from being sold into concubinage. Still, they could be removed from the novel without serious damage to the major story lines. The episode in which Chia Huan deliberately spills hot wax over Pao-yü's face not only illustrates the unhappy relationship between the half-brothers, resulting in part from the family's doting on Pao-yü but creates further tender sympathy for Pao-yü during his convalescence; the episode, however, adds nothing beyond a deeper understanding of Pao-yü's position through a contrast of characters.

Besides these scenes which relate to or further the story lines, there are several scenes that stand alone as interesting sequences of action but are not integrated into the novel, except, as we shall see, to recall or repeat other, relevant episodes. Stories such as that of Hsüeh P'an's wife, Chin Kuei, and her violent death by poisoning, or Yu San-chieh's display of pride and her consequent suicide, are interesting for the psychological insight they offer, but are essentially decorative, another nuance of the Chia disintegration. And the repetition of the poetry club meetings and the various poetry-writing contests, which are of little literary value, might be eliminated with advantage to the novel's total coherence, although they suggest the family pastime and the general Chinese interest in occasional verse.

Within each scene, the narrative makes broad use of detail, spreading the novel horizontally by diffusing the emphasis, as does the tendency to repeat information for the benefit of newcomers to a scene (even though the reader is already aware of it), which we have also noted previously. The liberal use of conversational dialogue, often including the repetition of polite greetings and appropriate responses, too, contributes to this feeling of leisurely diffusion and ties the novel to the unsophisticated oral background from which it emerged.

Indeed, if we look again at the date of composition, we realize that *The Dream of the Red Chamber* closely resembles the episodic "novels of manners" characteristic of the eighteenth and nineteenth centuries in the West and popularized by Fielding, Smollett and Thackeray, whose plots focus on the amorous adventures of some young hero during the course of his education into "polite society." Other parallels immediately come to mind—for example, Galsworthy's trilogy on the Forsyte family or any of Dickens' novels (in which social tract is transparently disguised in the form of a novel and certain characters become archetypes for the social and moral conditions in industrial England). These comparisons serve only to broaden our understanding of the Chinese epic, which unlike its Japanese counterpart, was not markedly influenced by Western imports. In other words, *The Dream of the Red Chamber* is one of those "large, loose, baggy monsters" that Henry James decried. Nevertheless, for sheer weight of incident, character and detail it is an extraordinary chronicle of life in Peking during the Ch'ing Dynasty.

If the organization is loose and highly inclusive, this structure reflects the experiences and perceptions of the author Ts'ao Hsüeh-ch'in, whose family history so closely parallels that of the Chias in the sudden dwindling of their sizable income through gross mismanagement of monies and spending well beyond their means.

Coherence is achieved through the narrative device mentioned earlier, i.e., the book is supposedly a record of the visit of an immortal to the Red Dust, witnessed and written down by a "mangy" Buddhist monk and a lame Taoist priest. Therefore the account is impersonal and scrupulously detailed. Some elements of myth, both in setting and character, which fall outside of the physical, human world, are included, but because they are subordinate to the main lines of the story, they do not negate the general, characteristic human reality of the book. Rather, the mythical sequences and the comments and actions of the monk and priest set the concrete standard of reality—in terms of moral value—against which the episodes and characters in the novel are opposed or measured. The force of the narrative is ironical, partly because the "narrators" serve a comic function in the plot, and partly because the scrupulous and lavish detail are, after all, "wasted" on an apparently unworthy subject.

The surface of this massive and complex book is like a fine filigree, spun out of minutely described ceremonies, dress, dialogue, landscape and action—the most polished facade that words can create without once going beyond the level of externals, to probe into the motivations and inner feelings, which in many cases are denied by the characters themselves. This surface narrative, then, is a perfect mirror of the moral life of the novel. The emptiness and shallowness of the characters, their strivings and dreams, or worse, their pretensions and rottenness of spirit, are cloaked in conventions. As individual personalities disintegrate, the breach between the personality and the social facade grows wider and more apparent. The novel is unified by a constant tension between a view of the "something-else-which-might-be-the-case" (the "real" world proposed as a norm) and the mortal world we see riddled with artificialities, a tension between the here-and-now, and the immortal that transcends all boundaries. This tension injects an underlying frustration and bitterness in the novel, probably an accurate reflection of the author's response to his circumstances (see note 3, Introduction).

If we draw back from the novel, we see that it is not molded and smoothed out by commentary, which fills in the crevices and holes and binds the parts together. The pattern is formed almost solely by the positioning and connecting of the two main stories and other relevant and less clearly relevant characters and incidents, to the central subject, the disgrace of the Chia clan. The pattern resembles the concept popular in Shakespearean times, of the Great Chain of Being, whereby the universe was conceived as a series of concentric spheres and disruption in any one sphere spread to all the others with violent reverberation. So, in the Chia family, injustices and corruption, even in the lowest quarters, affect the fortunes of the entire household until the situation grows so unstable that external forces must be called in to reorder the events. The episodes flow in a casual aggregation, and thus the surface of hundreds of finely wrought, individual characters and incidents, seems somewhat disjointed and irregular.

(3)

Characters

ALL OF THE characters in *The Dream of the Red Chamber*, perhaps with the exception of the supernatural ones, are highly individual persons living in Peking, under the Ch'ing Dynasty, during the eighteenth century. Each of the characters—over four hundred of them in all—is made concrete and distinctive through descriptions of his or her dominant traits. The degree of individuation varies widely, but the procedure for penetrating the levels of personality, through objective description and through dialogue, remains constant. Their physiognomies, dress, mannerisms, attitudes, and daily activities are carefully scrutinized, as well as the peculiarities and deviations of each character. Most of these minute details are noted through the eyes of one character or another, either in a meeting between two individuals or in the course of conversation with a third person, and those observations are then borne out by the character's own utterances (sometimes thoughts spoken aloud) and behavior.

Hence, as we concluded in the preceding chapter, from the beginning of the novel the characters live and reveal themselves through their interactions rather than through an omniscient narrator, and what the reader knows about each is what the characters tend to see and react to in each other, always, of course, filtered through individual expectations and societal conventions. At times the narrator does interject words or phrases that color the action, suggesting how or why a particular event occurred. For instance, the reactions of Pao-yü and Pao-ch'ai to Tai-yü's chiding of one of the maids for neglecting her mistress' instructions reveals something about the postures of each: "Pao-yü, when he heard this, knew Tai-yü was using this opportunity to teach him a lesson, but he said nothing and merely smiled. Pao-ch'ai knew this was typical of Tai-yü and paid no attention." In the Kuhn translation this practice is extended by the translator's addition of an occasional clarifying comment or by his choice of a more active verb than appears in the original. For instance, Pao-ch'ai "retorted" rather than simply "replied" to Pao-yü regarding the possible loss of his poems by Tai-yü during her journey (see Kuhn, p. 321). "Replied" would be closer to the original Chinese.

The detailed handling of a vast number of characters, however, is facilitated largely by the delineation of a few typical traits and symbolic associations, which are then refined and amplified through contrast between pairs of characters in order to develop the individuality of a certain character or point up his didactic function. In effect, each character emerges first through a series of epithets. Pao-yü quickly comes to mind as the Matriarch's favorite, the boy born with a magic jade in his mouth, or the spoiled, effeminate son of Chia Cheng. Likewise, Tai-yü is typified by her petulance and melancholia; Pao-ch'ai by her moderation and good sense; and Wang Hsi-fêng, by her cleverness, pride, and jealousy. Every character has a tag which elicits a memorable image: Liu *Lao-lao* is the country bumpkin; Hsi-jên, the devoted maid; the Matriarch, the doting, autocratic grandmother; Chia Cheng, the Confucian father-master, etc. Each corresponds to some general character type in Chinese fiction with the result that many of the associations are familiar and allow the reader's imagination full play in supplying details.

While the importance of certain characters depends upon the traditional hierarchies in Chinese society—age, position or place in the household, and participation in offices and rites—there are several who fall into a more fluid category in the novel. These characters enter the story in minor positions—the waiting maids, Hsi-jên, P'ing-erh, or Ch'ing-wen, or the still more obvious case of Liu *Lao-lao*—but make an impact through their vivid personal qualities or unselfish actions that gives each a memorableness beyond her specific function in the narrative.

Tai-yü is the most totally feminine of the characters, whose delicate physique is constantly being clarified by juxtaposing her with the more hardily feminine Pao-ch'ai. In her first introduction, she is described as ". . . so delicate that she seemed scarcely strong enough to bear the trifling weight of her clothing. And yet there was in her transparent, pale face a curious shimmer of voluptuousness and love of life" (Kuhn, p. 25). Whereas Pao-ch'ai is rosy and robust: "in her soft, rounded beauty, Pao-ch'ai resembled a smoothly polished, glistening agate. But her perfect polish was not only physical" (Kuhn, p. 41). Their temperaments, too, are different and, often, at odds. Tai-yü is feminine in the type of the jealous *femme fatale*, while Pao-ch'ai's femininity is subsumed in a maternal quality. As these two cousins mature into womanhood through the central experience of love for Pao-yü, the fate of each revolves increasingly around her relationship with the young Chia master and future heir. The focus of their development in the novel, then, lies in the emotional life of each girl, which has been prematurely affected by the death of one parent in childhood.

Upon the death of her mother, Tai-yü succumbed to her grief, a sense of being left alone and unprotected.[1] Her father tried his best to attend to her needs, but he too was stricken by the loss and furthermore as a busy official was forced to leave the child first in the care of a tutor, and later in that of her maternal relatives. Thus the burdens of everyday living tend to cower her, and Tai-yü is haunted constantly by thoughts of her own mortality, that she will die without the love she craves:

> Look! Spring is waning; and one by one the flowers
>   are falling.
> Now also will the radiant maiden age and die.
> Some morn when spring has departed and the maiden
>   grows old,
> The flowers will fall, the maiden die—
>   Neither knowing of the other.
>
> (Wang, p. 219)

Tai-yü identifies in the flowers, the epitome of transient beauty, all her ambivalent feelings. She desperately craves love, but fears at the same time that any love will, like her mother's, be taken from her, that the loved one will leave her. Therefore, her defenses are developed at the expense of her compassion, which finds a curious outlet in the care and attention she lavishes on flowers, burying them in flower graves she had prepared, lest they be defiled in death:

"It's good that you have come! You can help me to sweep up these flower petals and throw them into the water. I have already thrown in quite a lot," (Pao-yü) said.

"You should not do that! Here the water is tolerably clean, but later on when the petals have drifted farther along with the current, and float into other estates, they will come in contact with all kinds of dirt and refuse. It would be a pity for the lovely, pure petals to become soiled. No, it is better if we

take them to the petal grave which I have just dug behind that
hill. . . .

(Kuhn, p. 174)

These flowers symbolize her vulnerability, her need to
be protected. Like her, the flowers are exquisitely delicate and at the mercy of the elements.

Tai-yü's need for love and her great insecurity absorb
all her energies in self-pity and fits of temper, and it is
through a series of small, unimportant incidents that her
character is unfolded. The larger events of the household
do not concern her. She relates everything and everyone
to herself, ignoring or forgetting events or persons that
do not touch her personally. (Her behavior seems infantile, as if fixated by her mother's death.) Her standing
apart from major events in the Chia household corresponds with what she considers to be her peripheral
position there: she sees herself as an outsider, taken in
merely through kindness and family obligation.

When she enters the Chia quarters, she anxiously accepts the love and favors lavished on her by the Matriarch, Pao-yü and her aunts and cousins, as a substitute
for the love she has just lost by the untimely death of her
mother. Her whole idea of love stems from the mother-
child relationship, and it is this same protectiveness and
indulgence which characterizes her relationship with
Pao-yü, who nurtures her as a Crimson Flower in their
pre-incarnation story, and who appeases and consoles
her after each outburst following some real or imagined
insult with which her life seems fraught. Similarly, she
is softened by the Matriarch's loving welcome and generous treatment of her, by Pao-ch'ai's special attentions
when she is ill, or by the promise of Pao-ch'ai's mother,
Hsüeh Yi-ma, to treat her as her own daughter. Still, her
fear of rejection causes Tai-yü to see others as a threat to

her well-being, and she impulsively defends herself in the only way she knows how, by striking out cruelly against the person she loves, whose withdrawal of love, whether real or imagined, threatens her; this action is followed by her recoiling deeper into herself, lamenting her miserable state and growing ever more self-absorbed. Her sharpness and irritability are brought out by such things as her jealousy over Pao-yü's apparent warmth toward Pao-ch'ai, by Hsiang-yün's unthinking bad taste in likening Tai-yü to the young actress, or by Pao-yü's seemingly ill-bred reference to her as the heroine of *The Western Chamber*, who has a clandestine love affair with the hero.

Throughout the novel Tai-yü appears more acted upon than acting, always eliciting an extreme reaction by her unpremeditated outbursts. Those close to her— Pao-yü, her waiting maid Tzŭ-chüan, and Pao-ch'ai— understand the source of her moodiness and tend to comfort her. The others, who know only her volatile exterior, tend to judge her more harshly, seeing her as a piece of "black jade," and never penetrating the surface to discover her softness and utter helplessness. Like the prophecy of the Crimson Flower repaying love with tears, Tai-yü's fears are self-fulfilling, and the family does finally reject her as Pao-yü's bride. She dies a victim of their plans, unable to protect herself against the ordinary pressures of life intensified into this cataclysmic dashing of her hopes. Even on her deathbed she fails to realize that Pao-yü truly loves and suffers with her—a realization which might have provided her with relief, but more importantly, might have allowed her to express human compassion.

In comparison with Tai-yü, Pao-ch'ai seems colorless and predictable. The death of her father and her brother's demonstration of irresponsibility force Pao-ch'ai, as the perfect filial daughter, to take upon herself the management of the household, even though it means she must discontinue her studies:

Thanks to her great zeal for learning and to the care her late father had bestowed upon her education from earliest childhood, she was ten times better educated than her brother, Hsüeh P'an, who was her senior. But when she realized that her widowed mother could expect no real help from her ill-behaved elder child, she had laid aside her books for the past few years in order to relieve her mother of the household worries. . . .

(Kuhn, p. 41)

Her reaction epitomizes the difference in Pao-ch'ai's and Tai-yü's approaches to life and accounts for Pao-ch'ai's precocity, apparently the result of early responsibilities.

Pao-ch'ai appears an intelligent and dutiful girl, endowed with an infallible sense of rightness: it is she who always knows the right thing to say and the right moment to caution others with a quiet nod. She is totally practical, concentrating on whatever situation is at hand and capable of making adjustments. These qualities gain her immediate favor in the Chia mansions. She is frequently called upon to act as nurse, peacemaker and comforter, especially among her cousins, who, in their petty quarrels and self-indulgences, seem far younger than she. Pao-ch'ai also takes a more active part in family affairs than either Pao-yü or Tai-yü; she is the extrovert, revealing herself through her service to others. Armed with understanding, compassion and mental balance, Pao-ch'ai copes with a number of hardships that might embitter or destroy a weaker person, as they do Tai-yü, for example: her brother's thoughtless and criminal actions, her mother's reaction and consequent illness, Tai-yü's sharp jealousy of her, and finally, her mishandled marriage to a man who does not love her and who does little to hide his inconsolable disappointment that she is his wife.

Until this last event, we are inclined to see her, despite her virtues, as a trifle dull and plodding, always doing exactly what is proper and virtuous. This impression is reinforced by Pao-ch'ai's self-effacing attitude and her shunning of all personal adornments, which is perhaps best illustrated in the description of her austere chamber. The undecorated room lacks any of the rich, soft furnishings she might so easily have placed there—a room symbolic of her uncluttered heart, apparently free of self-interested desires.

On entering the pavilion the Matriarch felt as if she had been transported to a snow grotto, so drab and inhospitable did the interior appear to her. Not a bit of decoration, no curios, and no knicknacks. Only on the writing table a simple pottery vase with some chrysanthemums in it. The green gauze curtain above the bed, the few cushions and covers, were of the simplest kind. A few books and tea bowls completed the scanty equipment. The Matriarch sighed.

(Kuhn, p. 257)

As she attempts to cope with her marriage, however, Pao-ch'ai reveals the inner conflict between what she would like to do and what she knows she ought to do to save the situation. Faced with a set of difficult alternatives, she attempts to understand Pao-yü, who is consumed by a lasting love for Tai-yü, and to live with the responsibilities invested in her by the family, as Pao-yü's wife, rather than leave him. Her steadfastness increases the reader's awareness, earlier glimpsed in scenes of Tai-yü's abusive confrontation where Pao-ch'ai keeps rein on her feelings, that her virtue is not automatic. She exercises constant control in order to conform her behavior with Confucian teaching.

This restraint in every aspect of her life, however, stunts Pao-ch'ai's emotional growth, and her inability to express love as a personal feeling (apart from filial piety or serviceable action) is highlighted by the failure of her marriage. However much Pao-yü's rejection of them may cause her to question her total acceptance of the learned values of Confucius, in the end she solidly reaffirms them. C. T. Hsia has translated a scene of a conversation between Pao-yü and Pao-ch'ai, not translated in either of the two English versions, which illustrates the tragedy of their conjugal relationship, in which neither can meet the other on the same moral or philosophical plane.

After seeing Madame Wang off, Pao-yü began to study "Autumn Floods" [a chapter in *Chuang Tzu*] with minute attention. Emerging from the inner chamber, Pao-ch'ai noticed his exultant absentmindedness; she walked toward him to see what he was reading, and then her heart became very heavy. She thought, "He persists in regarding 'escape from the world and detachment from humanity' as his only concern; this is not good." Knowing it would be useless to dissuade him in his present rapt state, she sat down beside him, watching him intently. Finally noticing her presence, Pao-yü asked, "What are you staring for?" Pao-ch'ai replied, "It just occurred to me that since we are man and wife you are my lifelong support, even though I agree this relationship is not necessarily built upon our selfish feelings and desires. As for glory and wealth, they are but like fleeting smoke and cloud. But I am thinking that since the time of the ancient sages it has always been stressed that one should cultivate his 'moral character.'" Pao-yü didn't have the patience to listen to the end; he put aside his book and said with a smile, "Just now you mentioned 'moral character' and 'ancient sages,' not knowing that what the ancient sages have stressed is the importance of 'not losing the heart of a newborn baby.' What's so precious about the newborn baby, except that he has no perception, no knowledge, no greed, and no envy? Once we are born, we all get sunk deeper and deeper in the mire of greed, hate, and passion; how can we ever escape from the net of red dust? I have just now realized that the ancient saying, 'Whether we are together or apart, what we enjoy is but a floating life,' has awakened but few. As for one's moral character who has ever reached the condition of living in a state of primordial antiquity?" Pao-ch'ai answered, "Since you mentioned 'the heart of a newborn baby' you must know that the ancient sages regard loyalty and filial piety as characteristic of the heart of the newborn baby and not escape from the world and detachment from humanity. Yao, Shun, Yü, T'ang, the Duke of Chou, and Confucius all ceaselessly set their hearts on helping the people and benefiting the world, and the so-called newborn baby's heart finally amounts to 'not being able to bear the pain and suffering about me.' Just now you spoke of being able to bear the pain of forsaking the basic human relationships—what kind of absurdity is this?" Pao-yü nodded his head and smiled, "Yao and Shun did not force their way of life upon Ch'ao Fu and Hsu Yu, nor did King Wen and the Duke of Chou force theirs upon Po I and Shu Ch'i. . . ." Not waiting for him to finish, Pao-ch'ai retorted, "Your words are getting more and more absurd. If in ancient times Ch'ao Fu, Hsu Yu, Po I, and Shu Ch'i had received universal approbation, how come people today still revere Yao, Shun, The Duke of Chou and Confucius as sages? Moreover, it's even more ridiculous to compare yourself to Po I and Shu Ch'i. Victims of the declining fortunes of the Shang, they faced many difficulties and so they thought up some excuse for leaving the world. Now under the present beneficent reign, our family has for generations enjoyed Imperial favor, living in splendid style and luxury. Not to say that all your life your late grandmother, your father and mother have all cherished you like a precious jewel. Just think, is it right for you to maintain all that you just said?" Pao-yü took all this in but made no reply; he only tilted his head and smiled.[2]

In this scene Pao-ch'ai expounds the Confucian ideas for which she is spokesman in the novel, and which under-pin her stoical nature.

In closer analysis, Pao-ch'ai and Tai-yü represent opposite extremes of selflessness and selfishness, the one possessing those virtues that the other lacks. Tai-yü has neither self-control nor compassion; she is impatient for love, insecure about keeping it, a dreamy, intellectual type of girl. Pao-ch'ai abounds in self-control, sympathy, a sense of duty and conviction, but seems deficient in personal feelings and unable to project beyond her pragmatic view to contemplate the meaning of life and the unknown. Both women end up essentially unchanged in their outlooks, except that the possibilities hinted at in each of their personalities, which fail to develop fully in the course of the novel, make them seem pathetic. Tai-yü dies, her hopes desolated, while Pao-ch'ai is deserted by her husband and left to the work of rebuilding the Chia household from the rubble into which it has fallen. The implication is that neither Confucian nor Taoist doctrine holds the complete answer to life in the Red Dust. Tai-yü is too sensitive for the pressures of conventional society. She longs only to be free, to join with the man she loves solely on the basis of their love for one another. Pao-ch'ai, on the other hand, is unequal to the rampant evil of the mortal world, which is too complex for her, armed only with a finite sense of goodness, either to comprehend or cope with.

This same conflict between desire and duty that is essentially at issue between Pao-ch'ai and Tai-yü is explored also in two other characters, Chia Cheng and Wang Hsi-fêng, who not only represent contrasting extremes, but also offer many points of comparison with the two girls. Like Pao-ch'ai and Tai-yü, Chia Cheng and Hsi-fêng are shown to have personality traits which remain submerged under the form of behavior each adopts. However, the reader tends to see the latter two in deeper relief—in more absolute terms, and therefore as more functional characters—because of their age and position in the household. Whereas Pao-ch'ai and Tai-yü act according to temperamental affinities, it would seem that for the older adults the choice of a mask has been much more deliberate, or rather, that it has become so habitual that whatever provided the original motivation—education or expediency—seems long-forgotten, and the enforced pattern of behavior has become automatic, an end in itself. In other words, Chia Cheng and Hsi-fêng act out of compulsion, and with seemingly less self-awareness than either of the girls. Moreover, the focus in the life of the young cousins, as we have noted, is the vicissitudes in their love for Pao-yü—an emotional issue; while, for Chia Cheng and Wang Hsi-fêng, the focus is altogether different. Since it is they in whose care the management of the Yungkuo mansion rests, and who therefore are largely responsible for the fate of the family, it is their actions that have greatest consequence in the novel. Chia Cheng and Wang Hsi-fêng, then, must be judged on moral grounds, according to the consequence of their actions. The need for the reader to make this kind of judgment renders them less sympathetic characters than either Pao-ch'ai or Tai-yü, whose actions have little effect on the eventual outcome of the novel but do have considerable romantic interest.

Throughout the novel, Chia Cheng's commitment to what he sees as right is total. Possibly his code could be summarized in the sentence: We must follow the Confucian ways and bring honor to our family and ancestors. He is never motivated by personal gain nor concerned with the consequences of his actions as long as he deems them to be correct. In this respect he is unique among the male members of the family. The others are far more fallible, and the tension between their true motives, desires and actions, and their outer pretensions is much tauter. Generally Chia Cheng appears a stereotyped Confucian character, and only once are we made aware of the depth of emotion within him, over which he exerts rigid control in order to present a proper, conventionalized view, even to those closest to him. This scene takes place during the visit of his daughter Yüan-ch'un to the *Ta-kuan-yüan*, when Chia Cheng addresses her through a folding screen that shields the Imperial Concubine from the view of any man:

"The poor peasants who live on salted cabbage and dress in shoddy cotton are better off than we are," lamented Yüan-ch'un through the screen. "They can foster and satisfy their natural desire for family life to their hearts' content. But we, on the contrary, though we are made of the same flesh and blood as they, have to endure sorrowful separation. What good to us are all of our splendors and riches?"

Her father too was on the verge of tears, but he spoke words of comfort to her and exhorted her not to quarrel with fate, which had treated her so well, but to acknowledge with gratitude the favor granted to her by the Son of Heaven and to repay it with redoubled dutifulness.

(Kuhn, p. 139)

Chia Cheng's goodness causes him to suffer a great deal; it is also tainted by ineffectiveness and by a kind of officious seriousness that estranges him from his intimates. When he is appointed Corn Treasurer in the provinces, for instance, his righteousness leads directly to his inability to do the job and, of course, to his removal and demotion. At home too, Chia Cheng's rigid Confucian stance casts a gloom over the entertainment of the Matriarch and her grandchildren, notably during a contest in the writing of riddles:

The interest of the Imperial Concubine in the traditional pastime of the season made the Matriarch decide to conduct a contest of her own. . . . Noting his mother's high spirits, Chia Cheng also decided to be present and do what he could to please the Matriarch. However, his presence had the effect of discouraging everyone's gaiety and conversation, especially Pao-yu's, who usually enlivened the Matriarch's dinner table. Therefore, after three rounds of wine, the Matriarch suggested that Chia Cheng should retire early.

(Wang, p. 183)

Chia Cheng equates his duty as a father with his unceasing supervision of and emphasis on Pao-yü's preparation for the Civil-Service Examinations. Such devotion seems tyranny to his son, Pao-yü, who trembles at any summons from his father. Even the Matriarch remarks on his harshness, accusing him of punishing Pao-yü at the instigation of Yi-niang, Chia Cheng's jealous concubine, whose son, Chia Huan, is less favored by the family. Chia Cheng's most dramatic act, his beating of Pao-yü, carries no hint of the conflict between paternal love and duty which he must feel, but rather is executed with no visible wavering in his commitment to what he believes right. Thinking to chastise his son only so that he will bring no further disgrace upon his family, Chia Cheng recovers his usual control as soon as his righteous temper has subsided:

"Let him die! But do you think at all of the old *Tai tai?*" wailed his wife [Wang Fu-jen]. "As it is, she is not well on account of the hot weather. The death of her grandson will break her up completely!"

"Do not worry! In begetting and bringing up this degenerate whelp I have failed sufficiently in my duty. I have always, alas, allowed myself to be talked around by you in the past and have refrained from giving him this long-deserved chastisement. But today that is at an end. It is better that the young cur should breathe his last now than that he should live to do still greater harm later on."

(Kuhn, p. 243)

His view of goodness, while orthodox, is extremely narrow, and it bars him from any awareness of the larcenies and lies being perpetrated under cover by the members of his own family. Therefore, it would seem that even when Chia Cheng takes a stand in some ultimate sense, as he does in punishing Pao-yü, his energies seem misdirected, and the evils around him are much more prevalent and corrosive than he can conceive. Like Pao-ch'ai's, Chia Cheng's devotion to Confucian teachings—morally and ethically desirable as they appear in the abstract—do not serve him well as tenets for everyday life. While he represents the purest example of the Confucian *good* man, he is not strictly "nice."[3] He is rather an ineffective administrator, unable to cope with the corruption of the times and the circumstances in which he lives, as well as an insensitive person and severe father, behaving with a stiff rigidity that detracts from his character and renders him often cruel, thoughtless and inept.

Hsi-fêng, at the other extreme, verges on amorality. She is the pure type of the wily and powerful woman, beautiful, proud, and utterly ruthless, whose position is always somewhat precarious, and whose influence depends upon her maintaining the illusion of power, of goodness, and of absolute social correctness. Her actions are as carefully calculated and controlled as Chia Cheng's, but for opposite reasons. Hsi-fêng is wholly motivated by self-interest. She always knows exactly what is to be expected in any social situation and ingratiates herself to those from whom she can gain by captivating them with her beauty, charm and talent. She makes

a point of condescending to those below her, intimidat-
ing all but a few with her power, and increasingly, with
the threat of beatings or exposure. Her rise to power
begins with her supervision of the Ningkuofu during
the funeral services for her nephew-in-law's wife, K'e-
ch'ing, and continues on an upward sweep until her
illegal business dealings are uncovered in the course of
the search of the mansion.

Though her rise to power and sudden plunge from it
are interesting to watch, they are never surprising to the
reader. Her choice of actions is based undeviatingly on
personal advantage or recrimination. For instance, one
of her first official orders as mistress of the Ningkuofu,
and the deliberate means by which she establishes undis-
puted authority, is to sentence a servant to twenty lashes
and the loss of a month's wages for being late for roll call.
Her acts of kindness, such as letting the Matriarch win
at *mahjong* when she is obviously losing, or visiting those
who are ill and ordering special food or medicine for
them, are all transparent attempts to keep her reputation
spotless and her position of leadership unchallenged and
they are clearly offset by innumerable cruelties. In fact
Hsi-fêng's actions are connected with a series of deaths
throughout the novel, which in some way reflect on her
abuses: the death of Chin Ko, whose engagement she
undertook to buy off at the request of the Abbess of the
Water Moon Convent and who then committed suicide
rather than be unfaithful; that of Chia Jui, whom she
thoroughly punished and humiliated for his attempts to
seduce her, and then refused the expensive medicine that
might save him; that of Pao-erh's wife, who hanged herself after the discovery of her affair with Chia Lien and
the beating given her by Hsi-fêng; that of Yu Erh-chieh,
who was harrassed to a death by her own hand as a result
of Hsi-fêng's slander and gossip. Hsi-fêng is also respon-

sible for trying to kill Chang Hua, whom she ordered Wang-erh to do away with, though he did not carry out her order.

There is no time when Hsi-fêng thinks unreservedly about another person. She remains under all circumstances concerned with herself. Even at the end of the novel when her fall has brought her to the bottom of the pile, her remorse is based solely on her own disgrace and loss of face, and given the chance to regain favor, she shows no sign of a moral conversion, but rather a persistence in her crafty ways:

A visit of consolation to Hsi-fêng on her sickbed formed the last gentle rumble of the storm, now finally abated, which had swept over the family. Hsi-fêng held her breath in terror and, covered with shame, hid her head under the bedclothes when she saw the Matriarch entering her room, accompanied by Wang Fu-jen, Pao-yü and Pao-ch'ai. Conscious that she was the chief cause of the financial ruin of the family, she had been prepared for a merciless storm of abuse. She believed the favor of the Matriarch forfeited forever, and was wishing for nothing but a speedy death. Instead of the reproaches which she expected, however, she not only received comforting words but was loaded with all kinds of useful presents as well as three thousand ounces of money; all this thanks to the fact that her secret money manipulations had been so considerately kept from the knowledge of the Matriarch. As her mind was set only on worldly possessions and prosperity, the improvement in her position immediately renewed her spirits. She performed her kowtow of thanks with astounding cheerfulness and agility in her bed and promised that in future she would work and strive for the Matriarch and the family with all the industry of a kitchen maid.

(Kuhn, p. 549)

In this regard, Hsi-fêng resembles Tai-yü, who never understands her position clearly enough to realize that

[72]

a change in her behavior would be not simply acceptable, but also safe; and therefore, both die at the point in the novel where their actions would only effect irrevocable destruction.

The attempts to resolve the conflict between duty and desire are manifest in every character, and it would seem that the individual resolutions reflect significant differences in age, temperament and moral commitment. The youngest generation, just emerging from childhood, are in the process of formulating or internalizing moral values by means of an emotional commitment, as we have seen in Tai-yü and Pao-ch'ai. The second or adult generation, exemplified by Chia Cheng and Wang Hsi-fêng, tend to react much more mechanically: although they offer elaborate rationalizations for what they are doing, they really show in their actions the degree of moral commitment each feels. The oldest generation, represented by the Matriarch and Liu *Lao-lao*, form the link with the once great and noble past of the Chia family. Although their lives are nearly spent, these two characters retain much of their original vigor and authority, and thereby act as a constant reminder of the weakness and corruption of the younger generations. Each of them has come to terms with her own situation and is living out life more or less complacently, expecting the younger generations to subscribe scrupulously to a code of ethics to which they, as elders, pay only lip-service. The purpose of this code is not to tax the mind severely, but instead to provide a set of strict social forms which will serve both to relieve the necessity for constant moral deliberations, and more importantly, to protect these older people from further suffering and distress in their last few years. Accordingly, the contrast between the Matriarch and Liu *Lao-lao* centers on social behavior; and in fact they do belong to two distinct social classes or rankings, each lending a very different tone to the narrative. For this reason, the Matriarch and Liu *Lao-lao* contribute a special "felt-life" of their own, and the scenes in which they appear are among the most vivid in the novel.

The Matriarch is the typical Chinese grandmother, ruling over two or three generations gathered under one roof, proud of her family, indulgent to her favorite grandchildren, always sure that her generation was stronger and more active than the present, weak one. Her rule is autocratic but also kind, softened by her understanding of human nature and her avid enjoyment of life's luxuries, especially of good food and theatrical performances.

On the twenty-first a small stage was set up in the Matriarch's court and a troupe of actresses was hired for the occasion [by Wang Hsi-fêng who dutifully attends to the Matriarch's pleasures]. It was entirely a family affair and no guests were present except for Hsüeh Yi-ma, Pao-ch'ai and Hsiang-yün. When Pao-ch'ai was asked to name what she wished to see, she refused the honor at first but yielded at the Matriarch's insistence and named a scene from Monkey Sun, as she knew that the Matriarch liked plays with plenty of action and acrobatics. The Matriarch was naturally delighted with the performance.

(Wang, p. 179)

She loves ceremony and festive occasions, always taking delight in the entertainment at such family gatherings and joining in the young people's games with a relaxed good humor that belies her age. For the Western reader, whose family structure may differ radically, the Matriarch is almost a comic figure. But for the Chinese reader, I suspect, she represents a familiar, beloved stereotype.

She is presented essentially from one angle—as absolutely dedicated to her family and convinced that she knows best how to teach them to live properly and enjoy life, i.e., by adhering to tradition. There is no question of duplicity within her. Her total lack of malice and the fact that she is purposely kept blind to the declining circumstances of the family and to the failings of her favorites (Pao-yü and Wang Hsi-fêng), by some who want to spare her the worry and by others who want to avoid her interference in their affairs, make her seem a sympathetic and somewhat foolish old woman. She, after all, claims for herself more responsibility than she is willing to supervise closely, being more attentive to her own diversions, and delegating the money and duties to others in the household, principally to Hsi-fêng. The nightmare search of the mansions and the arrest and exile of her son and grand-nephew cause the Matriarch much anguish and disappointment. Despite these feelings, she remains firm in her convictions, but now plagued with remorse and self-doubt, believing she has failed to communicate these traditional values to her family:

"O Mighty Heaven up above us! I, of the family of Shih, the unworthy head of the Chia clan, humbly lay myself at Thy feet and implore mercy of Thy divine majesty. Throughout many generations my race has striven to keep to the path of virtue and not to turn to the ways of evil. As far as lay in my power I have endeavored to be a devoted wife, mother, and grandmother to my husband, children, and grandchildren respectively. Even if I cannot claim to have done any outstandingly meritorious work, neither can I accuse myself of any outstandingly wicked deeds. In consequence of the arrogant, dissolute, and sinful mode of life of some of the younger descendants of our illustrious ancestors, the race of Chia has fallen into disgrace and ruin. A son, a grandson, and a great-grandson have to expiate their crimes in prison. I take the blame for all the evil, because I failed to give them the proper training. Now, O Mighty Heaven, I implore Thy gracious protection and support. Have pity on my children and grandchildren! Let me atone for them by a speedy death! Punish me and spare them! Turn their sorrow into happiness, their mourning into joy! . . ."

(Kuhn, p. 546)

This prayer, and the division of her own personal goods among her relatives when she learns of their impoverished state, affirms the fundamental optimism of the dying Matriarch, who accepts without question the reinstatement of Chia Cheng and the rising curve of fortune signalled by his brother's forfeited title being conferred on him.

Though her death occurs soon after these events, little is made of it in the book. It is neither dramatic nor tragic. It is the natural aftermath of a full life and comes quickly and quietly. She seems in her life and death to illustrate perfectly what Muir has said of the pure character as opposed to the dramatic or changing one: ". . . it is of their life, and of that alone, that we are aware, not of their life and death, not of that double fate which colours all dramatic figures. The true character seems to exist equally in all time, and untouched by time."[4]

Liu *Lao-lao* is the same type of steadfast, sympathetic character. Although she appears in only a few brief scenes, they are memorable for her good-humored acceptance of her lot. Like the Matriarch, she has a strong sense of family duty and a clear-cut morality. She is essentially a pragmatist, who goes to ask help of her rich relatives when her own family is in need, then returns with the produce of a good harvest to repay the Chias, who have now fallen on bad times themselves. Her direct, moral impulse again asserts itself when *Lao-lao* prevents Hsi-fêng's daughter from being sold into concubinage.

[76]

If she plays her role with simplicity, Liu *Lao-lao* does not do it without a great deal of self-awareness and warm humor. True she appears ridiculous in the scene where she is invited to dine with the family, her awkward manners providing ample entertainment, a scene which has afforded the Chinese, whose language is rich in sayings, with another. Any country bumpkin out of his element in sophisticated society, or by extension, anyone out of his depth in any social situation, merits the comparison, "Like Liu *Lao-lao* entering the *Ta-kuan-yüan*." And she is equally comic in her fierce pride in her own constitution when she boasts later in the book that she has a full mouth of teeth, all in good condition except for a loose left molar. In both of these scenes, however, it is apparent that Liu *Lao-lao* enjoys her own buffoonery and that she willingly clowns for the sake of the Matriarch, a woman of about the same age, who suffers from ill-health and a nervous disposition. For example,

> After the meal they took a siesta in T'an-ch'un's bedroom. The waiting maid Yüan-yang stole along to Liu *Lao-lao's* side and asked her not to be offended at the tricks they had played on her at table.
>
> "What is there to be offended at?" replied Liu *Lao-lao*, laughing. "I took part in them of my own free will and play-acted for your Matriarch, in order to cheer up her old heart a bit. That was all arranged beforehand with Madame Hsi-fêng. When I am really angry I am in the habit of keeping my mouth shut."
>
> (Kuhn, p. 255)

What she does, then, she performs with full knowledge and acceptance of the possible consequences: "I am old and more thick skinned and it won't hurt as much if I get my face slapped" (Wang, p. 63). The consequences for Liu *Lao-lao* are not related to her morality, only to her social position; and she more than anyone is aware of the limitations imposed by her lowly status, which stands in opposition to the Matriarch's exalted one:

> "But we are born to labor while Lao Tai-tai is born to enjoy the blessings of Heaven. . . . What would become of the farm work if we were like Tai-tai? . . .
>
> "That [eating, sleeping, and diverting herself with the company of her children and grandchildren] is Lao Tai-tai's blessing from Heaven. . . . I would like to do those things but I can't."
>
> (Wang, p. 276)

Both women have an ironic view of their own situations, as the scene in which they discuss their health and pleasures indicates. Therefore they believe that in living by a simple, traditional code and doing the best each can, Liu *Lao-lao* through hard, physical labor, the Matriarch through a flurry of parties and household activities, each will have fulfilled her moral duty. Since, in defining duty, both women take into account their own limitations, or weaknesses, they tend to understand the excesses of other characters, to bear sorrows admirably and to forgive. Neither of them is considered above humor or below seriousness; both are specific, individualized characters who nonetheless represent general, and in this case highly diverse, social types.

By rejecting the Red Dust and its responsibilities, Pao-yü is the only character in the novel who undergoes a moral conversion and thereby attains immortality. Through a process of growth and education he learns that the choice between duty and desire is not a "real" decision, but rather one imposed on humans by the "unreal world" in which they live. It is through the emergence of Pao-yü's intellectual powers that he arrives at this moment of enlightenment. This point is important because among all the characters who figure in major roles in the novel, Pao-yü is the only one whose societal function depends directly upon intellectual achievement —upon his passing the Examinations—and he is the sole character, with the exception of his half-brother, Chia Huan, whose mental ability is in question. He does poorly in school, frittering his time away on "worthless" novels, occasional verse, and escapades with his male companions; and he appears unstable emotionally, with his childish outbursts and depressions and his predilection for feminine playthings and company.

Pao-yü's final actions, however, are consistent with the symbolic framework of the novel, foretold from the pre-incarnation story and the parallel tale of Shih-yin at the beginning, and in a number of dream sequences and meetings with the priest and monk that are connected with the powers of Pao-yü's magic jade. Furthermore, his choice has a precedent in the Chia family in Pao-yü's uncle, Chin Lao-yeh, who relinquished his claim to the Ningkuofu in favor of his son, Chia Chen, in order that he himself might enter a Taoist retreat. The reader tends to see Pao-yü on two separate planes, however, and it is not until the end of the novel that his earthly and supernatural selves merge in a single fate. Because of the minuteness of many of the incidents which affect him and the great variety of people with whom he becomes involved, Pao-yü's growth is neither obvious nor quick. Rather, on a superficial reading he seems unchanged for a good portion of the novel, retaining his characteristic compassion, warmth and feminine sensitivity.

From his first appearance, when he is introduced to Tai-yü, Pao-yü is seen as a delicate, perfectly formed, twelve-year-old boy who, pampered and spoiled by his grandmother, is given to frequent tantrums and to coming and going as he pleases. As a result of this treatment he remains infantile, conceiving of himself as centrally important. His self-centeredness is reinforced by his grandmother's doting, his mother's inability to discipline him, and his favored place among his girl cousins. In feminine company he therefore has ample outlets for his sensitive feelings, but as yet no effective curbs on them, since his father's curbs are occasional, short-lived, and essentially ineffective. Tai-yü's personality is equally if not more sensitive than his own, and her presence motivates Pao-yü to exercise control over his feelings, not out of fear, as he does with his father, but for love. His realization that he must quell his selfish impulses if he is to develop his relationship with Tai-yü comes slowly, with frequent lapses on his part, but gradually he contains himself more completely, and this ability grows with the deepening of his love. Eventually Pao-yü learns to think of Tai-yü's feelings first and to act in harmony with them, if necessary concealing his own sensitivities in order to protect her.

While he is often wild and difficult as a child, Pao-yü is also capable of great sympathy and generous acts, evoked by the slightest suffering in another. His adolescence unfolds through incident after incident in which he expresses kindness or comes to the aid of a friend, or, conversely, takes offense and withdraws, hurt by the smallest innuendo. Both reactions may be attributed to this same sensitivity, and indeed, it is his emotional life which is developed in the earlier part of the novel, as Pao-yü concerns himself with the problems of those living in the Chia household and a few whose connection with the Chias is only tenuous. He commiserates deeply with the actress, Ou-kuan, whom he barely knows, for instance. When he accidentally comes upon her burning paper money for her dead lover, he promises to have incense burned himself in honor of the boy's memory. In the absence of his waiting maid, Hsi-jên, he takes personal care of Ch'ing-wen, the maid who is taking her place and who has contracted a cold. Pao-yü prescribes and administers her medicine and even procures and applies ointment for the patient's headache himself. Later, he visits her in her bleak room after she has been unjustly dismissed from service and ministers to some of her last wants. Pao-yü is also affected by the deaths of various young persons who fall ill or die by suicide. Remembering them all sympathetically, he performs rites in honor of the dead Ch'in Chung, Ch'in K'e-ch'ing, Ch'ing-wen, and Chin-ch'uan. The threat of his maid, Hsi-jên's, departure causes him a night of anguish, and at the suggestion that Tai-yü is to be married and sent away he suffers an almost total mental collapse. Then, too, it is Pao-yü who suggests that the aristocratic nun, Miao-yü, give Liu *Lao-lao* the cup out of which the latter had drunk instead of allowing it to be thrown away because it had been defiled, as the proud girl intended. In all these acts Pao-yü demonstrates his tender and compassionate nature, his interest in all those whose lives touch upon his own, especially in their suffering.

This interest, when seen in relation to Pao-yü's male friends, carries obvious hints of homosexuality, an impression supported by his effeminate inclinations, his exchanging intimate gifts, and such incidents as his skirting of his father's direct questions concerning the actor with whom he is reported to be intimate, an action which leads to his violent beating. While the theme of homosexuality is common in the Chinese vernacular novel, signalling the folk origins of the genre and adding a bit of lewd humor to the plot, the suggestion of Pao-yü's homosexuality seems veiled, perhaps associated with human excess in earthly life (recalling the accusation of the Goddess of Disillusionment that he is the most licentious of men) or the idea of his belonging to an unnatural breed. From a strictly psychological point of view the homosexual tendencies may be accounted for by the domination of females in Pao-yü's life and the dread influence of his father, whose rigid Confucian ethics Pao-yü finds impossible as a model for his own behavior; and insofar as the homosexual may be considered a self-centered person, this theme would account for Pao-yü's gradual withdrawal from his emotional bonds. Still, the scenes of Pao-yü in male company are always somewhat ambiguous and less brilliant than those he shares with his girl cousins, as well as less central to his character; the boy clearly prefers the presence of females.

The emotional side of his personality is well developed up to the time of Pao-yü's marriage, after which he begins to close in upon himself in an irreversible retreat. His marriage and the circumstances accompanying it— the deception followed by the sudden, lonely death of Tai-yü, and the moving away of his former companions —cause a basic change in his character. All of his sympathies are bound up in his loss of Tai-yü, and Pao-yü becomes apparently impervious to the sufferings he inflicts on Pao-ch'ai, his grandmother, his mother and others around him. As C. T. Hsia points out, Pao-yü is faced with a tragic dilemma: "Is it better to suffer and sympathize, knowing one's complete impotence to redeem the human order, or is it better to seek personal salvation, knowing that, in achieving this, one becomes a mere stone, impervious to the cries of distress around one?"[5] The reader is carefully prepared for Pao-yü's choice of the latter alternative by such incidents as the loss of his stone and the final dream in which he learns the fate of the girl cousins and maids who formed part of his life but are now remote.

Following his talk with the mysterious monk who returns his lost jade, Pao-yü determines to extricate himself from earthly bonds, in which his sensitive and sympathetic nature has enmeshed him, and to regain his former status in the world beyond the Great Stone Arch, where he was a self-sufficient being. This he does at the end of the novel when he goes off into a mist, arm-in-arm with the Buddhist monk and the Taoist priest. The moment symbolizes Pao-yü's approximation of the Taoist ideal of non-being and thus is consistent with the moral and symbolic framework of the book, exemplifying the author's ambivalence toward the Buddhist and Taoist traditions. Just as Chia Cheng, in representing the strongest Confucian character, illustrates the ineffectiveness and callousness of such an extreme position; so Pao-yü, at the moment of his renunciation, embodies the frivolous irresponsibility of the other doctrines. In both instances the ethical framework of the novel seems to interfere with the character development. The radical change in Pao-yü's personality strikes the reader as perhaps contrived, although his highly developed sensibilities and his position as family heir make Pao-yü's gesture paramount in the context of Chinese thought.

The shift in Pao-yü's attitudes is reflected in his changing relationship with Chia Cheng, whose attempts to regulate the boy's intellectual activities culminates in Pao-yü's passing the Civil-Service Examinations, a measure of his mental growth. Chia Cheng's effect on Pao-yü is unlike that of any other character in the novel: in his presence the relaxed Pao-yü becomes stiff, the self-assured companion becomes the panic-stricken son. Chia Cheng's summons elicits cringing obedience and a cowering fear. Pao-yü's encounters with his father tend to be explosive, from their initial scene where he bids Chia Cheng good-bye and tongue-tied, receives a verbal blast, to his fearful but more assured, even cocky answers during the tour of the *Ta-kuan-yüan* when mottoes are being composed. This last scene shows the early recognition of Pao-yü's intellectual talents by those who make up the company, and of his father's secret esteem for his older son, betrayed in Chia Cheng's constant urging of originality and his calling the boy back after he has cut him off and sent him away abruptly. Still, Chia Cheng's anger is more apparent than his pride in this scene.

Much later in the book, when Pao-yü's father examines him in order to evaluate his readiness for marriage, there is a shade of change in their relationship. This scene does not appear in the Wang translation and is drastically cut in Kuhn, but in the original there is a discussion of some points of view expounded by Pao-yü, drawn from the Confucian *Analects*, where father and son for the first time seem to meet in an atmosphere of calm rationality. Chia Cheng begins with the apparently sincere purpose of examining Pao-yü objectively. His remarks are unemotional, based on what Pao-yü has written and not on any of his extraneous ideas or behavior, as had previously been the case; and Pao-yü has produced not a poem but a serious commentary, part of the schoolwork that Chia Cheng holds as important. The author has translated a portion of this scene as follows:

[Chia Cheng] read the second essay, the subject of which was, "Not to feel hurt because men do not recognize you." He first read the corrections Tai-ju had made: "A person who does not become hurt because he is not recognized, in the end will not lose his sense of contentment." He looked carefully at the crossed out words underneath, and said, "What did you say? 'One whose heart cannot be hurt, he alone is a scholar.' Your first clause is like the words of the theme, 'to not feel hurt,' but your last clause goes beyond the limits of the last clause of the original which defines a superior man; certainly if you change what is written, you must bring it into harmony with the topic in a proper way. The last clause must seek to clarify the first one, this is the law of good writing, and you must carefully comprehend it." Pao-yü nodded. Chia Cheng then read further on and saw: "Now an ordinary man cannot but be hurt when men do not recognize him; but with a superior man it is not so. As for a person who is happy though he is not permitted to speak, how can it ever be possible to reach this state?" The original ended with the words, "Is not he alone a scholar?" Chia Cheng said, "This part has the same mistakes as the part which broaches the theme. The corrections are all right, they make it clear and acceptable." (Chapter 84)

The development in Pao-yü's relationship with his father depends on the boy's reluctant willingness to follow Chia Cheng's academic bidding. Such a change is prompted by the dullness of Pao-yü's environment after his companions have drifted away from their garden residences, leaving him with fewer opportunities for entertainment and therefore, with a melancholy, dispirited feeling. Out of boredom and distress Pao-yü submits himself to academic rigors, not out of intellectual concurrence with his father, from whom he remains intellectually distant. The direction in which his father guides him coincides with Pao-yü's spiritual "travels" to his pre-incarnate state, where he will enjoy the freedom of spontaneity and non-artificiality.

Even granting a much greater rapprochement between Pao-yü and his father than may be evident, Pao-yü's final taking of the Examinations seems inconsonant with his character. It is true that he is no longer the pampered, self-centered Pao-yü, given to temper tantrums and to idle, girlish dallying with powder and rouge, yet his growth has not been in the direction of accepting the traditional family responsibilities, but rather toward disillusionment, coupled with a firm determination to quit the Red Dust. Since he ascribes no value to the Examinations, which is indeed incompatible with his beliefs, his taking of the Examinations can be justified only as a last homage to his parents, the symbolic fulfillment of duty to his family. Pao-yü actually makes this claim:

"Up till now I have had no opportunity of repaying my mother for all the love that she has shown me since I came into the world," he said earnestly. "I will exert myself to pass the examination as well as I can and thereby make good my former negligence. If it is granted me to give my parents joy by a notable success, I shall regard my filial duty as fulfilled and the injustice which I have been doing my parents all my life atoned for."

(Kuhn, p. 576)

As a last gesture, however, this one seems particularly weak and ironic in light of the basic duties as a husband and father-to-be that Pao-yü leaves unfulfilled with no apparent sense of guilt or regard for the future of the clan. The fact that Pao-yü passes the Examinations makes his disappearance that much more desolating because it robs the family of the honors. If anything, it represents a reversion to Pao-yü's earlier compassion, a wavering before his final departure, and the departure itself signifies a total control of all feeling and impulse, which have to some degree marked all his earlier actions. If we look at the completeness of Pao-yü's character, this final action seems to flatten him out suddenly to the author's didactic purposes, a deflation which flaws the total conception. This problem has been discussed by numerous Chinese critics, and those who feel it is a weakness of the novel generally attribute it to a dual authorship, i.e., the fact that Kao Ê, who completed the last forty chapters, either did not have or did not follow the suggested lines of Ts'ao Hsüeh-ch'in's narrative.

(4)

Time and Space in the Novel

A NOTHER ANGLE of vision in the criticism of structure is the analysis of the relative dominance of time and space. It is an approach developed by Edwin Muir in his *Structure of the Novel.* If the author, he says, sets a somewhat static scene and depends on the interactions of characters upon each other and upon the scene, triggered by the changes wrought in them by time for the development of his plot, the major structural base of a novel is time. On the other hand, if the author places his characters in numerous scenes, depending for the development of his story on a variety of backgrounds against which to place them and to which they react, the major structural base of the novel is space.

... the imaginative world of the dramatic novel is in Time, the imaginative world of the character novel in Space. In the one, this roughly is the argument, Space is more or less given, and the action is built up in Time; in the other, Time is assumed, and the action is a static pattern, continuously redistributed and reshuffled, in Space.[1]

The critic who approaches the structure of the novel from this view looks first at the story while the previous critical view required the examination of the characters.

... the plot of the dramatic novel is intensive. [It] ... begins never with a single figure, but with two or more; it starts from several points on its circumference, which is a complex, not a nucleus, of personal relationships, and works toward the centre, towards one action in which all the subsidiary actions are gathered up and resolved. [It], while not altering its setting, shows us the complete human range of experience in the actors themselves. There [character novel] the characters are changeless, and the scene changing. Here the scene is changeless and the characters change by their interaction on one another. The dramatic novel is an image of modes of experience, the character novel a picture of modes of existence.[2]

Forster, on the other hand, speaks not of this contrast between time and space in a novel, but of one between "the life in time and the life by values," using a slightly different approach and terminology, which, when analysed, comes close to Muir's space-time division between "modes of existence" and "modes of experience." "And what the entire novel does—if it is a good novel—is to include the life by values as well."[3] In his discussion of the difference between "the life in time and the life by values" as they are embodied in a novel, he emphasizes the unevenness of man's concept of his existence as it is modified by his experiences which gives him an image of "the life by values" based on experiences in time telescoped by intensity. In this concept, time is the dynamic element and space is incidental.

... there seems something else in life besides time, something which may conveniently be called "value," something which is measured not by minutes or hours, but by intensity, so that when we look at our past it does not stretch back evenly but piles up into a few notable pinnacles, and when we look at the future it seems sometimes a wall, sometimes a cloud, sometimes a sun, but never a chronological chart.[4]

Balzac, one of the novelists most committed to the importance of "space," of surroundings and environment as major forces in a novel, focuses on the alteration

[88]

of persons by space and of space by persons, with time as the common denominator of these changes.

Man is not alone but exists in society, in a social environment, and so far as we novelists are concerned, this environment is constantly modifying events. That is just where our real task lies, in studying the interaction of society on the individual and of the individual on society. . . . Once we grasp this, we see that social environment will be affected by all these human phenomena we learn to control. And in this direction lies all that constitutes the experimental novel: mastery of the mechanism of human events; demonstration of the way in which intellectual and sensory processes, as explained to us by physiology, are conditioned by heredity and environment; and finally portrayal of the human being in the environment which he himself has made and alters daily, and in the midst of which he in turn undergoes continual transformation.[5]

Though time, then, as these critics show, is a more dynamic element in a novel than space, an analysis of the way in which each of them is used in a novel, and of the contributions of both to the development of the "life by values," or to the demonstration of the "mechanism of human events," can provide some insight into the basic structure of a particular novel and its aesthetic whole.

In *The Dream of the Red Chamber*, "Space is more or less given, and the action is built up in Time." As we saw when we were examining the character structure, the circumscribed space in the novel forces the complex knot of character relationships to grow primarily from the changing attitudes of the characters which develop from their experiences with each other in time. Temporarily leaving aside the supernatural portions with which the novel opens, we see that we are introduced immediately to a sizable group of characters, all of whom face and affect each other in some way. This group continues to enlarge during the course of the story, always

looking inward, toward the center, but frequently shifting, cementing or severing relationships as the days and
years succeed each other. From time to time some characters drop out and others enter, but all stay generally
within the circular space allotted.

This space is limited essentially to the Chia family
compound, and most often, within this circle, to the
Ta-kuan-yüan, the garden where so many of the daily
incidents are played out. This narrow setting is obviously symbolic of the narrow outlook and homogeneous
influences which are characteristic of the Chinese family
life of the time. It is, as Muir has said, an "image of
humanity's temporal environment."

By what seems at first a paradox we shall find in the dramatic
novel a far more intense visual realization of the scene than in
the novel of character. No doubt this is partly because the
scene in the former becomes coloured and dyed by the passions of the chief figures, because we always see them against
it, and closed in by it. But it is more essentially because the
scene here . . . is not an ordinary and particular scene at
all, . . . but rather an image of humanity's temporal environment.[6]

The thoughts, experiences and attitudes of the major
characters of *The Dream of the Red Chamber* are all limited
and conditioned, as Balzac would point out, by this
physical environment and their lack of knowledge of
what lies beyond it. If, on one level, the novel can be
taken as a *bildungsroman*, the hero must learn his lessons
about life through intensity and repetitiveness of similar
experiences in a homogeneous environment, rather than
through breadth of contact with persons and places. Perhaps a valid comparison can be made between Hans
Castorp's education in the closed society of the Swiss
sanatorium in *The Magic Mountain* and Pao-yü's education in the closed society of the Chia compound. Each by

nature, but also because of his environment, reacts to delicate nuances and small modulations in characters and scenes that in a more open setting might very well go unnoticed. And each is penetrated—in his inner self and in his relationship with the physical and spiritual world around him—by intensely realized experiences with the people who touch him closely in a narrowly limited physical setting, chosen by Hans but forced upon Pao-yü by circumstances. Only occasionally do the gates of the compound open and the characters move outside into a different sphere of experience, contrasting and highlighting the usual scene. In *The Magic Mountain*, Hans goes down to the village or up to the snowy, desolate mountain peaks. In *The Dream of the Red Chamber*, Pao-yü goes out to the poor servants' homes not far away from the compound, to the Buddhist temple, to the convent or to the family burial place. Whenever the scene expands in this way the characters are given an opportunity to react without the social and psychological pressures which exist in their familiar environment, to a different background and changed surroundings. In *The Dream of the Red Chamber* this is perhaps most vividly evidenced during the funeral procession when the group stops at the home of a country family. Here each of the participants, but especially Pao-yü and Ch'in Chung, have an opportunity to turn away from the Chia mansions and away from the tight relationships and familiar conventions of their own closed circle to have a kind of "picaresque" experience, which the author presents as a first encounter with the values of the soil. The boys are decidedly affected by it. Pao-yü, particularly, is surprised and evidently delighted with his introduction to some of the basic principles of farming and especially with his instruction in the art of spinning. The scene, of course, highlights the affluent lifestyle of the Chia's by contrasting it with the thrifty and practical manner of country people, but it also represents a development in Pao-yü's "life by values," which has taken place by displacing him in space rather than by melting influences around him in time.

> He had never seen the various farming implements before. He did not even know their names, and had to ask the servants who were accompanying him to explain their use and purpose. When told, he could not get over his astonishment at the number of new things he was learning there.
> "Only now do I understand the meaning of the old proverb about the rice in the dish, of which every grain is the result of endless trouble and exertion," he remarked thoughtfully.
> (Kuhn, p. 106)

Each time he steps outside the compound to go to Hsi-jên's, Ch'ing-wen's, the temple or the convent, he is involved in a similar learning experience. Yet, despite these moments it is obvious, since the author so seldom draws him outside, that his world, and that of all the Chias is essentially a closed universe impervious to most such influences. And it is a world whose concrete familiarity becomes unconsciously imbedded in the reader's mind, after a while taking on a life of its own, informed by the characters who live in it and reflecting them.

> Setting is environment; and environment, especially domestic interiors, may be viewed as metonymic, or metaphoric, expressions of character.[7]

Familiarity soon makes us less conscious of the setting than when it is first introduced, and we settle into a kind of forgetfulness of it (except where it is specifically called to our attention), and concentrate on the individual characters. Yet it cannot be thought of merely as a static background against which developments take place. It has another function which represents a dynamic force in the novel and here it differs from the *Magic Mountain*, and from many dramatic novels with an undifferentiated scene. If we isolate the setting from the characters and view it as a thing in itself, we see that it has a kind of life of its own, represented by a rising and falling curve. The Chia compound is always impressive, but before the announcement of the visit of the Imperial Concubine, despite its elaborate essentials, it has no unique identity. Once the visit is known and the preparations for the *Ta-kuan-yüan* are set in motion, it takes on a new life, flowering in the magnificent garden, which symbolizes the height of the family's affluence, overextended but awesome. For the major portion of the novel this garden is a fresh place, alive with flowers, trees, birds and waters, which provides great enjoyment for the young people who live in it, with their laughter, chatter, and sometimes tears. But as the story progresses, it begins to reflect the declining fortunes of the Chias. A begonia blooms as an evil omen, the birds fly off, one by one the pavilions are deserted and stand bare. Eventually, unwanted ghosts come and turn the once-delightful setting into a place of terror. It has had its childhood, adolescence, maturity and old age. And, as with a living thing, when the garden—the heart of the Chia compound—dies, the whole body shrivels. We see then that, while space "is more or less given," the setting within the space mutates, adding its own element of change to the dynamic movement of the novel. Time is the major force in this process, imposing its changes on scene and character alike. Theoretically, according to Elizabeth Bowen, this double change should be ineffective.

Scene promotes, or contributes to, advance by its freshness. ... Frequent change of scene *not* being an imperative of novels

. . . how is there to continue this freshness? By means of ever-differing presentation. Differing because of what? Season of year, time of day, effects of a happening (e.g., with house, rise or fall in family fortunes, an arrival, a departure, a death), beholding character's mood. At the first presentation, the *scene* has freshness; afterwards, the freshness must be in the presentation. . . . Change should not be a factor, at once, in *both* scene and character; either unchanged character should see, or be seen against unchanged scene. Two changes obviously cancel each other out, and would cancel each other's contribution to the advance of the plot.[8]

Yet, instead of cancelling each other out, these two changes in *The Dream of the Red Chamber* reinforce each other, emphasizing on two simultaneous planes, spatially and in the depth of the human heart, the ravages of time. The dimension of contrast which highlights the growth and development of character against a flat, unchanging background is lost, it is true, but what is gained is a greater complexity of texture with scene and characters woven together in a common pattern, undifferentiated except for plane.

The Dream of the Red Chamber is, therefore, primarily an "image of modes of experience," since the plot of the novel is intensive, drawing the characters closer and closer together as the range of human experience unfolds in time. Yet because these modes of experience are played against a spatial background affected and developed by the same temporal influence, it is also, to a limited extent, a "picture of modes of existence" as well.

This is reinforced on another level where there *is* a major spatial change in the novel—in the supernatural portions. Interestingly, this change is extra-spatial, throwing the action into a void where space is supposedly immeasurable and time is inoperative. This is true both of the early segments of the novel, which take

place under the Nonesuch Bluff, and of the dream sequences. As we discussed earlier, however, the "Great
Void" is spoken of in highly concrete spatial terms, with
a geography and topography of its own, and therefore
this basically limitless area takes on somewhat arbitrary
limitations here, allowing it to be evaluated in spatial
terms. The supernatural segments are, then, basically
"pictures of modes of existence" such as we might find
in a novel with a highly differentiated scenic background, but set on a different plane of existence, intended by the author to represent a supernatural reality.
Because these scenes make use of the same cast of characters transported to another plane of reality, relating
them in ways reminiscent of, though sometimes in opposition to their existence in time, they become, to a limited
degree, "images of modes of experience" as well. As
such, they provide an interesting balance between the
dynamic forces of time and space which, when related to
the realistic portions of the novel, qualify to some extent
the basic structural dynamism of time.

This dynamism of time, which imposes change, is not
a simple mechanism in a novel, for not only the
chronology but the "feel" of time must be represented.
Tempo, the speed with which a novel moves through
time, and rhythm, the accent it places on certain events
by allotting them a larger proportion of the available
narrative time, are both correlatives of this problem of
showing the "feel" of time. The novelist might need to
indicate, for instance, that one span of time within the
story moves quickly while next to it a similar span moves
slowly, or perhaps that all time in this novel moves
slowly. Percy Lubbock speaks of this as representing the
form of time: "The form of time is to be represented, and
that is something more than to represent its contents
in their order . . . the lines and masses of the book

must show it."[9] Austin Warren speaks of it in terms of the difference between "fable time" and "narrative time":

Fable-time is the total period spanned by the story. But "narrative" time corresponds to "sujet": it is reading-time or "experienced time," which is controlled, of course, by the novelist, who passes over years in a few sentences but gives two long chapters to a dance or tea-party.[10]

Lubbock explains how Thackeray deals with the problem of indicating time-which-seems-not-to-move by paying no attention to sequential actions but building them in an apparently lateral way, returning back and forth across the same period to make a complex, dense texture of time:

. . . time, at Castlewood, is not movement, it is tranquility—time that stands still, as we say, only deepening as the years go. It cannot therefore be shown as a sequence; and Thackeray roams to and fro in his narrative, caring little for the connected order of events if he can give the sensation of time, deep and soft and abundant, by delaying and returning at ease over this tract of the past.[11]

Modern novelists have used time in innumerable ways as a structural element in a novel: moving it chronologically forward and backward, removing all perspective of its sequence as if all things were of the now in the present, or of the now in the historical past, combining the sequential movement of time with suspended time to form a complex psychological pattern that exists sometimes only within the mind of a character, and numerous other ways.

The representation of the "form of time" in *The Dream of the Red Chamber* has been seriously affected by the translations, both of which frequently have suppressed or compressed scenes or whole chapters in the interest of a novel of more readable length. Wang has more drastically altered the "feel of time" by his type of elision which abstracts the main lines of a scene, sacrificing many of the less important details of action, dialogue or description. Kuhn more frequently omits whole scenes rather than reduce them, retaining more detail in scenes he does translate, but both Wang and Kuhn alter to a certain degree the basic relationship between scene and summary. Time moves much more slowly in the original work, which contains a number of incidents and descriptive passages which add to the feel of time gliding slowly downhill but with increasing momentum. In both translations, because less material from the latter portions is translated than from the earlier ones, the feel of increasing momentum of action is over-emphasized toward the end, with one misfortune tumbling upon another at breakneck speed, a tempo which is somewhat slower and better paced in the original work.

The total "fable time" of the realistic portions of the book is probably between seven and ten years, covering such developments as the adolescence and early maturity of Pao-yü, Tai-yü, Pao-ch'ai and a number of the residents of the compound, the growth in power and sudden fall of Hsi-fêng, the rise, recession and reinstatement in public life of Chia Cheng, and the latter years of the Matriarch's life. The "narrative time" moves very slowly throughout the entire book because the author in the majority of cases chooses to dramatize rather than summarize, making frequent use of dialogue, and often repeating information for the benefit of new characters who enter a scene, even though this information is already known to the reader. (These repetitions are removed in both translations.) They perhaps represent a vestige of the oral tradition of storytelling out of which the vernacular novel grew, an art which demanded repetition as a mnemonic device.

This use of scenic presentation rather than summary very well may be another characteristic of the novel related to its roots in oral literature, since it is highly characteristic of the earlier form, which depended for its audiences on the storyteller's ability to dramatize vividly. This characteristic is also, as we mentioned previously, directly related to the concrete nature of the Chinese language, which both illustrates and influences the Chinese predilection to think concretely rather than abstractly.

Generally, the presentation of scenes in *The Dream of the Red Chamber* is chronological, with the line of time moving directly ahead, but at an almost imperceptible rate, often placing one dramatized scene after another in a fairly long chain before the rhythm is broken with a summary portion. Often a dramatized incident of three or four pages moves the story ahead only a few minutes of fable time because of the amount of detail. This detail, however, is not analytical or musing, such as we find in Richardson or Proust, for instance; it is generally a surface description of external things and a reporting of movements, gestures and dialogue. The following scene, one out of any number that might be chosen, will illustrate this kind of immediacy of narrative technique:

The next morning Ch'ing-wen awoke with a heavy cold. Her nose was obstructed, her voice was hoarse, her limbs were heavy and stiff. According to the rules of the household every illness, however trifling, had to be reported at once to the *Tai tai*, and the old *Tai tai*, who was very apprehensive about infection, was in the habit of getting sick servants out of the palace immediately and sending them back to their families. Pao-yü, already deprived of Hsi-jên, was unwilling to have the pretty maid Ch'ing-wen also removed from his vicinity. He therefore decided to keep her at home and to get a doctor for her, unknown to the Matriarch.

"But Madame Hsi-fêng at least should be told. Otherwise she may find out that the doctor has been here, and take it amiss that she has not been told about it," objected Ch'ing-wen.

Pao-yü agreed, and sent a serving woman to Hsi-fêng. Ch'ing-wen had caught a slight cold, it was nothing at all serious, and he begged—so the message ran—to be allowed to look after her at home as he could not well do without her; he would get a doctor in by the side gateway, and would she, Hsi-fêng, please not make any fuss about the matter. Hsi-fêng sent back word that she had no objection, but if there was not an immediate improvement the patient must definitely leave the house and go back to her family, for the danger of infection was particularly great in these winter days and the health of the young ladies was very precious.

"She really carries on as if I had the plague!" exclaimed the offended patient, peevishly. "Very well, then, I'd prefer to go away at once in order to save the grand ladies here from any more headaches."

She sat up and was about to start packing her things, but Pao-yü pressed her gently back on her bed.

"Do not be so quick to take offense!" he said placatingly. "Hsi-fêng feels responsible to the old *Tai tai*, and wants to feel that she has done her duty in case anything should happen, but she did not mean it so strictly as all that."

At that moment the doctor whom he had sent for appeared on the scene, escorted by three elderly attendants. Pao-yü hid hurriedly behind a bookcase. The serving women let down the red embroidered curtain in front of Ch'ing-wen's alcove, then the patient had to stretch her hand out through the curtain. The doctor looked for a while at the hand and the two fingers, the nails of which were two or three inches long and dyed red with China balsam. Then he felt the pulse after a serving woman had wrapped a clean handkerchief around the patient's wrist.

"Internal congestion, external irritation; a slight cold due to the bad weather." In these words he explained his diagnosis to the serving women when they got outside the door.

(Kuhn, p. 315)

This characteristic handling of surface detail slows the movement of time, but keeps it going in a generally horizontal line rather than stopping it in order to develop the story in depth. There are only one or two places in the whole of the original (several interpolated places in the translation) where the story line is totally halted for a commentary, and these are fairly brief. As an example:

Foolish girl! Foolish boy! Why were they shamming and saying the exact opposite of what was in the depths of their hearts? They had belonged to each other secretly long since. Why did they torture themselves and behave as if they were strangers and enemies? They were spiritually so close to each other. Why did they outwardly struggle away from each other? But alas, that has always been the way with lovers, and doubtless always will be.

(Kuhn, p. 221)

Pure descriptions of scene with no elements of time are also rare. The long descriptive passage about the newly constructed *Ta-kuan-yüan*, for instance (which is omitted from the Wang translation), is a good example of the author's usual introduction of an element of time into a description of scene, since the garden is described as it is being examined by a group moving through it on a tour of inspection.

Variations in tempo are hard to plot in a novel as long as this one. The first five chapters of introductory material are more uneven than the latter ones, quickly spanning a long period of fable time which passes before the major stories of the novel begin. Chapter 1 moves rapidly through a summary of several millennia between the Goddess Nü-kua's repairing of the Dome of Heaven and Chen Shih-yin's dream about the Precious Stone and how it came to be born into the Red Dust, which is told in great detail. The foward movement of the story is then stopped totally for a good part of the second chapter while the background and relationships of the Chia family are clarified during a long conversation between two minor characters. The next chapter resumes the sequential advance of earthly time, introducing the major characters and at the same time drawing a picture of the main setting by using as a technical device the entrance of Tai-yü into the Chia household. The fourth chapter continues this forward movement and the introduction of major characters by presenting the Hsüeh family, related to the Chias but not included in the family tree listed in Chapter 2. The fifth chapter then again stops time momentarily in order to introduce the stories and the possible fates of the twelve maidens of Chin-ling through the medium of Pao-yü's dream. The structure of these chapters, especially the summary nature of Chapters 2 and 5, eliminates the later necessity of explaining relationships as new characters are introduced. Chapter 5, too, serves to set up the stories of the maidens that will develop in time, although the cryptic nature of the poems makes them somewhat difficult to follow. (Neither translation includes many of the poems, which are hard to translate adequately.)

After these introductory chapters, the real tempo of the novel begins and continues, unhurried and pleasantly indolent, until the major misfortunes of the latter portions of the novel, which begin with the report of strange, nocturnal noises in the *Ta-kuan-yüan*. The passage of time is generally marked from day to day, sometimes skipping a period of "a few days," and more rarely of a few months, but there are no large lapses of time, from one year to another, for instance, which are unaccounted for by a series of incidental happenings. The early portions of the fable time, when the children are in their early teens, are more carefully detailed, as the relationships between the characters are being established and developed. Sometimes, as mentioned previously, the story is developed laterally with two incidents that are happening simultaneously explained one after the other, or with a brief flashback to fill in needed explanation for a developing story. This happens less often than one might expect in a story of this length, however, the predominant concept of time being clearly linear.

The novel's tempo is increased as the end of the story approaches, not because greater lapses of time occur between incidents but because fewer incidents and fewer details concerning the incidents are presented. In the earlier portions many of the stories merely develop the characters more fully or add to the general meaning of the novel, but have no specific function to move it forward. The latter portion of the book is leaner and less casual. Each incident is chosen for a specific action which moves the story on, and therefore the novel is quicker in tempo.

Besides tempo, another approach to time in the novel is to look at the rhythm, always a time concept, by isolating repetitive patterns, "the combination of the repeated and variable with the repeated as the ruling factors."[12] Local patterns of repetition with variation can be very simple, "combinations of word and phrase, sequences of incident, grouping of characters,"[13] often with the variation developing gradually so that the basic pattern becomes more and more complex and accretes more and more meaning from a succession of contexts. Forster used the "little phrase" in the music of Vinteuil in Proust to exemplify this process and comment on the function of rhythm:

A banner can only reappear, rhythm can develop, and the little phrase has a life of its own, unconnected with the lives of its auditors, as with the life of the man who composed it. It is almost an actor, but not quite, and that "not quite" means that its power has gone toward stitching Proust's book together from the inside, and towards the establishment of beauty and the ravishing of the reader's memory. There are times when the little phrase—from its gloomy inception, through the sonata into the sextet—means everything to the reader. There are times when it means nothing and is forgotten, and this seems to me the function of rhythm in fiction: not to be there all the time like a pattern, but by its lovely waxing and waning to fill us with surprise and freshness and hope.[14]

Rhythm is a difficult critical concept to apply to a novel. It is distinctly internal, originating in local patterns of repetition with variation, then growing and expanding according to its own principles to form a distinctive rising and falling current in the novel, roughly comparable to the irregular rhythms of prose, but almost never, in a well-written novel, to the regular rhythms of poetry or music.

There is one major architectonic movement in *The Dream of the Red Chamber* which dominates the entire work—the pattern of the rise and fall of the family. It builds like a large wave throughout the story, growing in intensity, size and power for more than half the book. Cresting at the seizure and search of the mansions, it gradually recedes and then builds again into a smaller swell. This pattern is echoed in several minor rhythmic segments where the motif of failure is repeated with variations. The stories of Ch'in K'e-ch'ing, Chia Jui, Ch'in Chung and the two Yu girls, for instance, all restate the major rhythm locally, showing the basic pattern of rise and fall, in reminiscent echo but not in exact repetition of it, therefore reinforcing it. The life of the garden, as we have previously pointed out, also falls into this movement of thesis-arsis-thesis.

This major rhythmic pattern is contained within the structure of the novel itself and is not treated symbolically or by repetition of images, words or phrases. There are, however, other incidental patterns of repetition or symbolic expansion which contribute to the total rhythmic foundation of the novel.

One image which takes on an immediate and developing symbolism is that of the tender flowers, short-lived and soon withered, and always associated with Tai-yü. She is established as a Crimson Flower in the first chapter (literally, Red Pearl Immortal Plant), and the use of flower symbolism in connection with her is obvious and consistent. It is, however, interestingly varied and is not invariably used when it might be expected. As Tai-yü first appears in the Chia compound, she enters through the flower gate into the world of her destined life on earth, and blossoms under the glow of her warm welcome and her acceptance into the life of her grandmother, Pao-yü and the other women and girls of the family. It is not until she has been there for some time, probably over a year (though it is hard to calculate exactly) that the motif of falling flowers is enuciated. The scene, quite central to Tai-yü and Pao-yü's relationship and to the development of the character of each of them, is both introduced and concluded with a reference to burying the fallen petals, the sad fate of which Tai-yü has carefully explained to Pao-yü who then shares her sympathetic concern. The scene, a part of which has been quoted earlier, opens with Pao-yü reading the play, *The Western Chamber*, one of the forbidden books his servant, Ming-yen, had bought for him. He is sitting under a blossoming peach tree whose petals are falling.

As he was sitting there and had just come to a place in the book which described "falling red, gathered up in heaps," a sudden gust of wind blew through the branches and caused a heavy rain of petals to ripple down on him and his book. He was covered all over with the reddish petals and had to shake himself to get rid of the delicate burden. So lovely and charming did these petals seem to him that he would have been sorry to tread on them with his feet. Therefore, he gathered up with both hands the rosy piles which lay round about his seat and carried them to the near-by bank, there to shake them over the surface of the water. And each time that he had shaken out two handfuls in this way, he remained for a while on the bank looking after the flower petals thoughtfully, as they danced about on the waves and were gently drawn by the current towards the weir.

Just as he was bending down to gather together another heap of petals, he heard a girl's voice behind him asking: "What are you doing here?"

He turned around. There he saw Tai-yü standing in front of him. She was carrying a spade over her shoulder, on the handle of which hung a flower carrier made of light gauze; in her left hand she had a broom.

(Kuhn, p. 174)

After he has noticed her, he invites her to help him sweep up the petals and throw them into the water, an invitation she rejects because she feels the petals would be carried by the current downstream where they would come in contact with dirt and refuse. Instead, she suggests that they bury them. They are distracted from their intention to bury the petals when Tai-yü discovers the book Pao-yü is reading and sits down to read it herself. An argument ensues when Pao-yü inadvertently compares Tai-yü to the heroine of the story, but after abject

[105]

apologies and a long and exaggerated oath by Pao-yü in which he promises never to say such a thing again, they make up and go to bury the flowers. " 'But now we will be sensible again and bury our poor petals.' They set to work again, and swept up and heaped the fallen petals and carried them to the petal grave behind the hill."

The symbolic meaning of the scene comes through in nuance rather than statement, relating Tai-yü to the flowers through her feeling for them, and opening through her a sense of compassion in Pao-yü. Later, how-ever, the flower symbolism is unmistakably stated in Tai-yü's poetic lament over her destiny to be like the short-lived, tender blossoms, fading soon after they bloom. The festival of Grain-in-the-Ear marked by the custom of saying farewell to the floral deities, occurs the day after Tai-yü feels she has been snubbed and turned out of the inner circle in the *Ta-kuan-yüan* when a maid has refused to let her into Pao-yü's cottage. Thinking it was Pao-yü who had given the order, she had turned away desolate, overwhelmed with loneliness and a feel-ing of exclusion. After weeping all night, she sets out the next day, overcome with grief, to bury more of her fallen petals. Wang, but not Kuhn, translates her Flower Burial Song.

> The flowers are withered, the flowers flown—
> flown across the sky.
> The red is faded, the fragrance faint—
> who is there to care?
> Wandering gossamers, lightly attached,
> float from the spring pavilion,
> And falling catkins, slightly damp,
> gently brush the embroidered screen.
>
> A maiden in her maiden's chamber
> mourns the dying of spring,

Her breast filled with melancholy thoughts
　　that can know no relief.
With a flower hoe in her hand
　　She emerges from the embroidered screen,
Loath to tread upon the fallen flowers
　　as she comes and goes.

The willow threads and elm blossoms
　　still flaunt their luxuriance,
They care not that the peach petals dance
　　nor that the plums are flown.
Next year the peach and plum
　　will bloom again
But who will be in the maiden's chamber?
　　Who knows? Who knows?

With this bag made of silk I shall gather
　　your fallen petals,
And with tender care bury them
　　under a mound of unsoiled earth.
You were pure when you came,
　　pure you may go,
Rather than fall into stagnant pools
　　or disappear into quagmires.

Now that you are dead and gone
　　I am here to bury you.
I wonder when the day will come
　　when I too shall die?
As I now bury the flowers
　　they laugh at my conceit,
Some future year when I am buried—
　　who knows by whom?

Look! Spring is waning; and one by one
　　the flowers are falling.
Now also will the radiant maiden
　　age and die.

Some morn when spring has departed
  and the maiden has grown old,
The flowers will fall, the maiden, die—
  Neither knowing of the other.

(Wang, p. 217)

Here the symbolic meaning is not merely through nuance, but through the juxtaposition of images so typical of Chinese poetry, clearly and unmistakably metaphoric. In the rhythmic expansion of this symbol it is the apex, after which come echoes and recapitulation, but never again such a clear statement. There are other references to the flower symbol such as that during the strained celebration of the Dragon Boat Festival when everyone is out of sorts with everyone else for various reasons and Tai-yü philosophizes about the painful fading of the flowers.

And so the banquet proved a most strained and tedious affair and everyone was relieved when it was over, but particularly Tai-yü. At no time was she very keen on social gatherings. The more pleasure people find in merry parties, the more keenly do they feel their cold and forlorn state when these parties are over; hence it is best to avoid such social gatherings altogether. Thus she philosophized. She thought of the flowers, whose fading was all the more painful the more one had enjoyed their blooming, and she felt it would have been better had they never bloomed. And so her face was mournful when other people had happy faces, and vice versa.

(Kuhn, p. 229)

And during a discussion later on during one of her illnesses, there is another echo and a veiled prophecy when she proposes to give Pao-yü the vase of flowers in her room. "I have an abundance of perfumes here already— medicinal odors. My drug vessel never leaves the fire the whole day. It would be a pity if the beautiful pure perfume of the flowers should be spoiled by these medicinal fumes" (Kuhn, p. 320). And finally it is suggested in the tragic scene when, on her way once more to visit the petal grave, she hears from the feeble-minded maid the secret of Pao-yü's marriage to Pao-ch'ai. She stumbles away distractedly, moving directionless, but always somehow being drawn back to the grave of the flowers.

> Lost in her thoughts, she moved painfully step by step, and at each step it seemed to her as if her legs were made of cottonwool instead of bones and sinews and had to bear a load of a hundredweight, so limply and flabbily did they do their work. Without goal or direction she dragged herself along, turning aimlessly and senselessly, now this way, now that, and so moving in a circle, with the result that she found herself back again and again in the vicinity of the footbridge near the blossom grave.
>
> (Kuhn, p. 486)

Interestingly, there is no flower symbolism in Tai-yü's death scene, where it might be expected to recur since this scene is the central picture of her as a tender blossom, faded and dying soon after it has bloomed. Though this lack avoids a certain obviousness in the symbolism, it also leaves this particular rhythmic pattern somewhat unresolved and may perhaps be accounted for less as an artistic reservation than as a result of the novel's dual authorship which sometimes interferes with the continuing unity of the book.

Though Pao-yü, like Tai-yü, has a basic symbolic equation (he is a Precious Stone), this figure is developed in a different way from the flower image. The flowers which symbolize Tai-yü exist separately and apart from her, with a life of their own, but the Stone is integrally and essentially connected with Pao-yü. He is born with it in his mouth, when he becomes ill he is cured because the wandering priest polishes it and miraculously renews its life-giving powers, when he loses it he becomes confused and irrational. The symbol does not expand, nor is it merely suggested in some places and stated in others. It is always a flat equation, stated periodically and related in varying ways with the surrounding texture, which makes it important in different ways at different times, but always providing a kind of accented periodic beat rather than a subtle variation on a previous rhythmic pattern.

There are numerous other local rhythms in the novel which contribute in various ways to making the total structural rhythmic pattern interesting and varied. These local rhythms are played out on the rising swell of the major wave, varying their incidental rhythmic figures from the even pattern of movement and development in the meetings of the poetry club or the family festival gatherings, for instance, to the syncopated rhythmic figures of such stories as Hsüeh-P'an's beating by Liu Hsiang-lien, or the abduction of the nun, Miao-yü, by a band of thieves. To trace all these figurations would be a laborious task, but it would provide an interesting analysis of the total rhythmic texture of the novel which is a complex of minor patterns prolonging and intensifying the major undulation.

A related critical approach, not confined to analysis of rhythmic structure, but often including it, uses as foci contrasts or balances among the various elements of a novel, such as scenes, characters, attitudes or views of life, playing each of them off against the other to find the basic negation, affirmation, or equilibrium. Knowing that in *Tom Jones* "natural man" is in the end triumphant, we can see the basic contrast as Dorothy Van Ghent isolates it:

In *Tom Jones*, life is conceived specifically as a conflict between natural, instinctive feelings, and those appearances with which people disguise, deny, or inhibit natural feeling—intellectual theories, rigid moral dogmas, economic conveniences, doctrines of *chic* or of social "respectability."[15]

Such contrasts or balances are not always two-dimensional. Separating foreground from background in a novel is one way of seeing them, though from this viewpoint the critic generally works with a continuum of gradation rather than a rigid contrast.

It is by perspective that our vision is adjusted. Without being placed in a perspective, any disproportionately exaggerated form would lack all meaning; it would be grotesque without significance. . . . Visual perspective is a matter of distinction between foreground and background, allowing for the perception of graded depths between them. We can expand the meaning of perspective so that it applies to events in time, to social phenomena, and to psychological and spiritual phenomena.[16]

Percy Lubbock gives an example of practical criticism based on such a view:

His people [Tolstoy's] move in an atmosphere that knows no limit; beyond the few that are to the fore, there stretches a receding crowd, with many faces in full light, and many more that are scarcely discerned as faces, but that swell the impression of swarming life.[17]

Contrasts are not always antithetical, nor are balances always equal. Often their value to the novel lies in a slight, unexpected imbalance where total balance might have been expected, and generally the resolution of a tension between contrasting attitudes is achieved through a final weighting of one of them. Having once fixed on the contrasts and balances within a novel, the critic must then notice and evaluate the contribution of these imbalances and weights to its structure.

In *The Dream of the Red Chamber* it may be easier to see some of the structural contrasts and gradations in depth if we see the story as a play. In the background is the supernatural scene which opens the story, set behind a scrim, a net curtain which is opaque when lighted from the front, transparent when lighted from the back. Back-lighted, the scene is clear and brilliant, showing Pao-yü as a Precious Stone centered between the Taoist priest and the Buddhist monk, who represent incarnate spiritual power throughout the book. In a "scene-within-a-scene," the story of the Crimson Flower and the Divine Stone Page is enacted and the pre-incarnation background of the story is brought to life, all behind the scrim. As Pao-yü steps into the brilliant light in front of the scrim to begin his earthly existence, the scene behind disappears and the "real" earthly setting appears, leaving the monk and the priest lost in the shadowy darkness. They later appear and reappear only when they are necessary to the story and without fulfilling the documented temporal or spatial requirements of reality so carefully kept for all of the earthly characters. It is as if the light behind the scrim is brought up periodically to indicate their presence and then dimmed again after the effect has been made and the reader is once more reminded of the real-unreal antithesis so central to the book. Pao-yü himself seems to step behind the scrim in the two dream sequences where he meets the other characters in a non-real way. This occasional shifting of planes in the novel provides a kind of structural device to keep the two foci of the story separate so that the final affirmation of meaning is clear. As in *Tom Jones* "natural man" is in the end triumphant, so here "supernatural man": at the end the lights are again dimmed on the earthly world of unreality and brought up for a brilliant moment of clarity on the real world of the "Great Void," then lowered again while the earthly world emerges into the now-dim lights of the final scene.

Besides such basic rhythmic and spatial contrasts, plus the major contrasts and balances in the figural structure which we spoke of in the last chapter, there are some subsidiary uses of contrasting or balanced characters which provide minor points of interest. The most common is the pairing off of two persons in the novel, generally but not always from two different levels in the basic family pyramid, so that one gets a statement of a character and a kind of mirror or echo as well. We find this kind of pairing in Pao-yü and Ch'in Chung for instance, where the latter is used as a kind of shadowy counterpart of the former. While Ch'in Chung lives, they are always together, Ch'in Chung by contrast clarifying Pao-yü and providing a foil for him.

It was inevitable that the two handsome, blossom-fresh young newcomers should very soon attract general attention among their fellow pupils, Ch'in Chung on account of his gentle, mild ways and his bashful, shy nature which made him blush like a girl when spoken to; Pao-yü, on account of his wealth and his self-assured bearing, his masterful behavior, his ease and skill with words.

(Kuhn, p. 68)

Ch'in Chung here, for instance, has absorbed the feminine adjectives usually used to describe Pao-yü and for the latter have been reserved uncharacteristic masculine terms, each character becoming consistently clearer and more three dimensional as he is outlined against the other.

In the original work there is an even more obvious pairing of Pao-yü with a young boy, son of a Nanking family, named Chen Pao-yü (homonym for "True" Pao-

[113]

yü in contrast to Chia or "False" Pao-yü), and an exact counterpart of him in every detail of appearance, attitudes and experience. From the time he was small, Chen Pao-yü liked the company of girls, and at one time had, like Pao-yü, fallen ill and nearly died, but had had a dream exactly like the latter's dream of the "Great Void" and had recovered and become a serious student. He was apparently intended to be the instrument for the return of Pao-yü's jade, but his actual contribution to the novel has become mutilated by the dual authorship, probably happily so since the similarities between the two boys seem grossly mechanical. Kuhn translates none of the portions concerning him, and Wang includes only a brief summary.

The Matriarch and Liu *Lao-lao*, whom we discussed earlier, are another pair of balanced and contrasting characters, often played off against each other, so that each becomes a more vivid individual in the light of the other, and both together provide a certain rhythmic repetition with variation in the overall continuity of the book.

The function of such sets of characters is partially structural, in a minor way, but more especially to develop the major character in the duo by throwing him or her into bold relief or by emphasizing minute differences in characters which are otherwise similar.

Other uses of balance and contrast include the continuum of gradation between the major characters in the foreground and the characters of varying importance who fill in the various levels of background in the novel. These, however, differ from Tolstoy's "receding crowd, with many faces in full light, and many more that are scarcely discerned as faces." The immediacy and surface nature of the narrative technique that we have spoken of earlier, gives each of these faces at least a momentary "place in the sun" and a brief moment of discernment as a face before it recedes into the crowd, so that the background of the Chinese novel is made up of discerned but forgotten faces.

The translator's selection process, too, alters the aesthetic pattern of time and space in the story. C. C. Wang makes of the book, despite its 564-page length, a clear story of the people who reside in the Chia mansions, emphasizing by suppression of almost all the detail of setting and of ritual the personal actions and relationships of the major characters, and especially the lovers. He retains almost all of the supernatural and philosophical material that opens the book but suppresses a good deal of the material at the end, making the preincarnation-incarnation-postincarnation story complete, but somewhat out of proportion, and making Pao-yü's final actions somewhat precipitate and philosophically unprepared for.

If the pattern of his translation were plotted into some sort of figure, perhaps it would be most similar to an inflating balloon. The story begins slowly in the "Great Void" with the mythical introduction and with the explanation about the tale being written originally on the stone and revised five times after it was transcribed. Once the major characters are introduced, the episodes in which they take part gradually expand the reader's knowledge of them, the air pressure of this expansion being essentially the personal actions and reactions of the characters rather than the influence of setting, environment or ideology, which are de-emphasized. When this expansion has reached its peak, the balloon explodes and, with the exception of a few fragments, the story is over. If we look at it quantitatively, the first five chapters are devoted to beginning the inflation by introducing the characters and the philosophical base of the story; the next fifty-two are devoted to telling the story itself, emphasizing the lovers and Hsi-fêng, who figure in the majority of the episodes selected. Then suddenly, after the marriage of Pao-yü and Pao-ch'ai in Chapter 57, the balloon explodes and all the fragments are gathered quickly into three chapters at the end, leaving the reader surprised that so many characters could be tucked away so quickly and so neatly.

Within the individual episodes the emphasis is on the dialogue between the characters, and a large portion of the book is told within direct quotes. Repetitions and polite phrases are removed as are most of the lengthy descriptions and allusions to literary, historical or philosophical material. Erotic scenes are minimized, and the plain language of the original is often euphemized. The pattern of two major stories emerges clearly with the weeding away of many of the minor and unimportant secondary episodes and the stripping away of allusive and descriptive language, leaving a feeling of leanness despite the number of characters and incidents that remain.

The book that emerges is an aggregation of episodes which are, in general, causally connected and which bring to immediate and forceful life the characters which people them. It paints them in such high relief, however, that the background from which they stand out is somewhat hazy, bringing the story close to the contemporary American scene at the expense of the feeling of a traditional Chinese setting.

Kuhn communicates a story heavy with the weight of Chinese tradition and conflicting Chinese philosophies, selecting from the original a combination of elements, both descriptive and narrative, which delineate the physical and social setting of the action. This emphasis on the background we see, for instance, in his retention of the lengthy description of the *Ta-kuan-yüan,* covering six or seven pages, and in the detailed descriptions of the ritual and ceremony of various times, such as the funeral of Ch'in K'e-ch'ing, or the visit of the Imperial Concubine. He also retains a number of passages in which the characters use historical, legendary or philosophical allusions (sometimes adding a clarifying phrase or sentence for the Western reader), and in which they discuss philosophical ideas, emphasizing thereby the particular tradition out of which the story grows. The result, since the story is always conditioned by the setting, is a complex of interlocking strands woven together to form a dense texture.

The specific pattern in the texture is often difficult to identify, though it is set in some relief by the actions of the major characters in the wave-like progression spoken of earlier. The individuals who emerge during this action do so, however, with a kind of halo-like effect, always accompanied by the social and ideological forces which produced them. Such an effect is accomplished by retaining the description of the ceremonial actions they perform, the clothes they wear, the utensils they use, etc., and—though the English is often awkward—the flavor of the language they speak. The following scene illustrates the meticulous retention of detail that ties the characters to the background. It begins just previous to Pao-yü's first entrance.

The meal was eaten silently and ceremoniously. From the swarm of serving women and girls, of whom some noiselessly carried the dishes in and out while others stood ready in the anteroom with washbasins, dusters, and hand towels, not the slightest cough or clearing of the throat was audible. Tai-yü had to be very attentive in order to adapt herself to the many forms of table etiquette which were new to her. For instance, perfumed tea was served immediately after the meal. She was about to drink it reluctantly, for at home she had always been taught that it was harmful to drink tea straight after a meal, but the example of the others soon made it clear to her that this tea was only meant for rinsing out the mouth. With the words, "You others may go; I wish to talk to our guest for a little while alone," the Matriarch rose from the table.

"How far have you gone in your reading?" she inquired of her grandchild.

"I have just finished studying the Six Classical Books," replied Tai-yü. "And what are my cousins reading?"

"Ah, they can barely understand a few words."

There was a crunching on the gravel outside, and immediately afterwards a servant announced: "Pao-yü is coming."

Tai-yü looked towards the entrance in eager expectation. Thereupon he walked in. She was most pleasantly surprised. He wore on his head a purple cap interwoven with gold and trimmed with brightly colored jewels. A golden band in the form of two dragons snapping at a pearl encircled his forehead. His close-fitting dark red jerkin, embroidered with golden butterflies and bright flowers, was fastened with a colored belt woven in a design of flower stems and ears of corn. Over the jerkin he wore a slate-blue satin Japanese cloak, embroidered with eight bunches of flowers, and fringed at the edges. His feet were enveloped in blue satin shoes. His face was as bright as the mid-autumn moon, his color fresh as spring flowers in the morning dew; his hair was as sharply outlined above his temples as if it had been cut with a knife, his eyebrows seemed as if painted on with India ink, the fine outline of his nose betokened boldness of character, his eyes glistened with the wet shine of autumn waves, his mouth seemed to smile even in ill-humor, and his glance radiated warmth and feeling even in anger. A golden chain in the form of a snake encircled his neck, and also a silken cord of five colors from which hung a beautiful stone.

(Kuhn, p. 29)

Sequentially, the story moves much as the original does, building to and from the same highlights. Because

Kuhn eliminates some of the unimportant, non-contributory scenes, as well as some of the less relevant ones, however, the texture of what he retains is more dense. The poetry-writing contests, for instance, are referred to only in passing summary, and all the scenes of the management of the mansion by the cousins, Li Huan, T'an-ch'un and Pao-ch'ai during Hsi-fêng's illness are suppressed. None of the sequences concerning the Chen family of Nanking are retained, and the several scenes of Hsüeh P'an's wife, Chin Kuei's attempted seduction of her husband's cousin, Hsüeh K'o, are combined in a brief summary of several paragraphs. In this suppression of scattered scenes and retention of elaborate detail in others, he emphasizes two major story strands. Pao-yü, Tai-yü and Pao-ch'ai are the major characters of interest in the first of the two, the love story, with the role of the maidservants as close associates of the lovers and a means of communication and influence between them retained and emphasized and the individual characters of the maids clearly developed. Hsi-fêng, the Matriarch, Chia Cheng, Chia Lien and other family members loom large in the second, the story of the rise and fall of the clan. The story of Hsi-fêng is not a separate entity against the background of the family decline, but the major focus in its disintegration, which has a number of root-like facets spreading through the story—Chia Lien's and Chia Chen's various sexual and financial disorders, Chia Jui's unfortunate end, or Hsüeh P'an's excesses, for instance, with the Matriarch and Chia Cheng's stability as a kind of standard of measurement for the dissoluteness of the others.

The pattern remains, however, an aggregate one with a voracious inclusiveness and spreading use of detail, as we noted above. Though some of the facets of the two stories become interwoven with each other, and many of the less-relevant scenes are integrated into one or the other of the major lines, others simply trickle out and end indiscriminately, the "recalcitrant material" of the novel refusing to be forced into a totally coherent pattern.

(5)

Moral View as a Controlling Force

If WE LOOK at the moral view of life which a novel presents, we can attempt to see it on one hand in terms of a controlling ideology to which all the parts are relevant, and on the other as an outgrowth of the prevailing religious and cultural influences which formed it. The simplest novels, in terms of this moral view, are those in which specified dogma controls the relationships between the parts. The critic, having identified the ideology and familiarized himself with its dogma, sees each piece of the novel fitting into its proper place in the overall philosophy. But such a single view often precludes more realistic, psychological development among the characters since it sets up a rigid pattern of causality that is defeated by too complex relationships among them. Evaluating a novel in terms of the culture out of which it grew, however, becomes more complex, since we are not dealing here with dogma or ideology alone, but with deep religious and cultural strains that spread into every aspect of life and action.

Any attempt to understand and evaluate the moral forces at work in *The Dream of the Red Chamber* and the patterns they produce, therefore, presupposes some initial understanding of the ethical, religious and cultural forces at work in the Chinese society of the time. Besides the purely folk elements, which do not figure broadly in this novel, there are three major streams of influence that thread their way through Chinese civilization up to modern times: Confucianism, Taoism and Buddhism.

The major influence through almost every age, of course, has been Confucianism which has predominated, officially or unofficially, for over 2000 years. Basically, Confucianism is not a religious doctrine. It is an ethical system based upon the need for men to devise some code of social values and behavior in order to live in harmony with one another. The system involves no belief in transcendence, in a supernatural being, in an afterlife. Confucius did not specifically deny any of these things—he simply was not concerned with them. Asked once if there were an afterlife, he replied, "How can I know about an afterlife when I don't know anything about this one?" His concern was man's relationship with other men and the problem of disharmony among them; this led him to emphasize the correspondence of inner attitude with external behavior in order to bring about harmony and mutually beneficial social relationships.

The ideal person, according to Confucian doctrine, is not the *saint* who excels in the perfect practice of the highest virtues, but the *gentleman,* who excels in the balance of proper attitude expressed in proper behavior, measured in primarily social terms. Its emphasis is on the training of a person to develop his *li*, or his inherited dispositions, and to govern his actions, especially those that affect others, by understanding his nature and by "the constant doing of what one ought to do in the universe as a 'citizen of the universe.' "[1]

The central virtues of the Confucian gentleman—uprightness, loyalty, human-heartedness, righteousness—are all concerned in some way with balance. Confucius was concerned that extremists of any sort would not fit smoothly in society, and that these extremes would, in turn, create a kind of disharmony.

Confucianism, then, was built upon a respect for relationship and balance, with the five basic relationships forming the pragmatic core of behavior. Having understood the need to be grounded in personal virtues, all of which are basically social in nature, the true Confucian needs to understand his place in the proper relationships which express these virtues: of ruler to ruled, of father to son, of elder brother to younger brother, of husband to wife, of friend to friend. These relationships all require mutual responsibility, a mastery of attitude and action, and a rigorous balance.

It is not difficult to see, given the social and ethical emphases of Confucianism, why it became a popular, sometimes state-supported cult. It encourages people to become good citizens and to obey authority. It sets clear lines and limitations and develops a fairly rigid set of expectations. It forms certain patterns of living, especially in terms of the family, that people can count on.

But it also is extremely vulnerable to the problem of formalism that can so easily beset any philosophy or religious movement as it spreads horizontally to the mass of a desirous but not discriminating populace. As Confucianism became more broadly accepted it became less thoroughly understood and too often identified merely with the external elements of behavior which were far easier to enact and to judge than the virtues they were intended to illustrate. Gradually these external rituals became unduly constrictive and rigid, leading to a kind of pervasive degeneration of the deeper meanings of the system; these in turn opened it to both manipulation and eventual reform. This pattern of growth, decay, manipulation and reform occurs throughout the history of Confucianism, making the understanding of it in any given time dependent somewhat upon the historical stance of the moment. It is not difficult to see the historical position of Confucianism on this continuum during the period of *The Dream of the Red Chamber* which concerns itself from the very beginning with the over-rigidity of the central Confucian characters.

It is against this milieu of an overly formalized Confucianism that Taoism is more easily understood, though historically they both appeared at about the same time in different parts of China. In almost total contrast to the rigidity and structure of Confucianism, Taoism provides no set of beliefs or program of action. It is not at all concerned with man's relationship to other men, but with his elemental relationship to nature.

The basic Confucian attitude toward man is that, while he is good, he can be made better by understanding and training and by learning how best to fit smoothly into his place beside other men. The basic Taoist attitude is that man is by nature good and that any attempt to educate him has the effect of distorting his natural conformity with life's processes, making him in reality less good than before. The *Tao* is essentially the way of nature, human and otherwise, and the true Taoist allows himself to be carried along by nature, never putting any barrier between himself and what he truly is. Taoist symbols include such things as water, which always seeks its own level and flows naturally without constriction, a doorway, the most important part of which is the empty space which allows freedom of movement, or a bowl, of which the most essential element is the space into which something can be poured.

While Confucianism places great emphasis upon man in his social relationships, Taoism champions the individual in his search for himself, insisting that this search can only come to fruition if man is utterly free to live as naturally as possible. The most characteristic Taoist aphorism, *"wu wei,"* is sometimes translated, "Do nothing and nothing will not be done." Do not educate, for when

you educate people you are making them over into something they aren't naturally. Do not form governments,
because when you form governments, you must force
people to do things in ways not natural to them. Allow
the goodness which is natural to men to prevail and
government, education and all other imposed social
forms become unnecessary.

The absolute Taoist is a hermit, living freely in peace
and tranquility, unconcerned with form or ritual. In
actuality, however, the number of pure Taoists in China,
because of the utter simplicity of its concepts which
require a profound understanding, has never been large
and the Taoism which has found its way into the popular
culture is a highly romantic degeneration of the concept
of the *Tao*. The pure philosophic form of Taoist thought
allows no room for dogma and no need for ritual. But a
growing mixture of Taoism with popular folk elements
and later with forms of popularized Buddhism developed a complex ritualistic religious cult, involving at
times such things as magic, alchemy, and exorcism, and
revolving around a priest-purveyor of ritual. Both the
pure and degenerate forms of Taoism are threaded into
the fabric of Chinese culture and both appear in *The
Dream of the Red Chamber*, the latter in the form of the
Taoist priest who constantly appears and re-appears
with talk of the magic stone, the former in The Great
Void which, in its purely philosophic form, is a concept
related to the symbols of the door and the bowl and the
sense that where there is nothing *created* there is everything.

There is a third religious and philosophic strain, Buddhism, which, though more recent than Confucianism
and Taoism and not native to China, must be considered
of equal importance as a contributor to Chinese culture.
The basic concern of Buddhism is that man be released

from pain and hence from the need to be reborn. Buddha's understanding of man is that his pain is caused by desire and that if he rids himself of all desire he can rid himself of all pain. Having once done this he has achieved *nirvana*, the perfect state of being without desire. Having achieved this the cycle of rebirth is broken and he is free.

Buddhism came to China from India and almost immediately touched the strain of Taoism there, with which it shares at least some superficial similarities of philosophy and ritual. There is a certain ascetic strain, however, that runs through Buddhism, at least in its original form, which is not present in either Confucianism or Taoism. Personal and bodily needs must be controlled if one is to rid oneself of desire, for instance—not a broadly popular stance in any age, and one which led to the development of a monastic form of life, which spoke both to personal holiness and to a communal sense of responsibility to lead the populace and show them how to live without desire so that they could eventually reach *nirvana*. In time, and with the inevitable popularization of the original beliefs of Buddha, dogma became less clear, a set of Buddhist saints or *bodhisattvas* developed, beliefs became culturally fixed, and Buddhism split into many sects and forms, each of which emphasized a particular element of belief or a particular form of ritual.

The popular, ritualized form of Taoism and several of the more popular and less ascetic forms of Buddhism developed alongside varied elements of the folk religions of China to make it oftentimes difficult to separate them in practice. In the novel the priest and monk invariably appear together and fulfill apparently the same functions. The strictly Buddhist elements of the novel seem weaker and less important than either of the others with

Confucianism obviously predominating until the somewhat ambiguous ending of the novel.

These three ethical and philosophical systems of thought are, to the Western mind, mutually exclusive; while we may understand how they can co-exist in a *culture* we find it almost impossible to accept the fact that they can co-exist in a *person.* Yet one of the major characteristics of the Chinese has been an ability to synthesize apparently contradictory elements into a comprehensive whole. This ability may grow from the Chinese tendency to deal less with theory than with the concrete and pragmatic (a tendency both illustrated in and influenced by the forms of the written language). The philosophical literature of China is filled for instance with parables and stories that are frequently accompanied by almost no explanatory text—the ideas are imbedded in the concrete picture. The line dividing theoretical philosophy and illustrative literature in China is in no way as clear as that which divides it in the West.

Understanding this de-emphasis of a need for a deeply comprehensive underlying philosophy may make a synthetic tendency of the Chinese more comprehensible to the average Western mind and help to build a deeper understanding of the kind of complex moral patterns that are possible when ideas are considered mutually enriching rather than mutually exclusive.

In *The Dream of the Red Chamber* the career of Chia Cheng, the most strictly and wholeheartedly Confucian character, exemplifies Confucian dogma at its clearest in his single-minded devotion to duty, his dedication to his family, and his intense sense of justice and responsibility. From his first introduction we are made aware of his interest in learning and his respect for the Confucian Examinations.

Chia Cheng, however, is a man of character and ability. From earliest childhood he manifested a fondness for learning. He was his grandfather's favorite. He intended to make a career for himself through the Examinations, but when his father died, the Emperor, as a special favor to the memory of a faithful courtier, exempted him from the customary requirement and made him an assistant secretary in one of the ministries.

(Wang, p. 25)

And in his relationship with Pao-yü we are constantly reminded of the importance he attaches to the Four Classical Books, the traditional and revered scriptures which contain the basic elements of the ethical doctrines of Confucius and his followers, rather than to the pursuit of poetry or art in such works as the *Shih Ching* or *Book of Poetry*. He is speaking here to Pao-yü's servant boy who accompanies him to school:

"And even if he knows thirty chapters of the *Shih Ching* by heart, that is still just as much vain noise and illusion as if a person who steals a bell were to stop up his ears and pretend to be dumb," he said. "Give my kind regards to the old schoolmaster and tell him not to waste his time teaching the *Shih Ching* and such antiquated useless rubbish; he should rather make them study the Four Classical Books so thoroughly that his pupils will know the text by heart from beginning to end. That is the most important thing."

(Kuhn, p. 67)

Though some of his actions are harsh and unfeeling and result in putting an unfortunate distance between him and those around him, they are morally irreproachable, and he remains a good and sincere man who in the end prevails, because the integrity of his character, honed by experience, promises better things to the clan in the future than have been true in the immediate past.

The author, then, has structured the novel so as to make the upward sweep of the suggested continuing story of the family converge in a person controlled by the dogma of Confucianism. Pao-ch'ai and her unborn child suggest a similar hope.

On the other hand, the Matriarch, who represents the highest Confucian authority, is one of the rare individuals who remain essentially immune to the pressures of dogma because her own personality asserts itself as more powerful than any other force. While Chia Cheng represents the legality and justice of Confucianism, she transcends such qualities in a warm humanity, commanding not only the proper ceremonial attention, but also the loving respect of her subordinates. In homage paid to her, therefore, the *ideal* of Confucian social relationships is crystallized, stimulated not by the desire to fulfill empty actions but by the desire to honor a worthy person.

She, too, illustrates this ability to recognize and act upon worth in others, even when this means stretching the rather strict conventions of propriety. This characteristic is most clearly evident during the visit of Liu *Lao-lao* who would be far from welcome in most aristocratic Confucian circles but who is made to feel very much at home by the Matriarch.

The Matriarch replied kindly to her exuberant greeting and asked her to sit down.

"How old are you now, Cousin?" asked the Matriarch.

"Seventy-five," replied the old woman, standing up briskly.

"So you are older than I am! See how healthy and strong she has remained!" said the Matriarch admiringly, turning towards the bystanders. "Who knows how decrepit I may be if I ever reach her years!"

"There must be distinctions; wise Providence sees to that.

Our kind is, after all, born for work, the old *Tai tai* for gentle living. What would become of farming without people like us?" said Liu *Lao-lao*.

"Are your teeth and eyes still sound?" the Ancestress asked, continuing her inquiries.

"They are in the best of order. Only a back tooth on the left side has become a little loose recently."

"What a useless creature I am compared with you!" sighed the Matriarch. "My eyesight is getting bad, my hearing is weak, my memory plays tricks on me. I avoid the company of strangers in order not to show my physical weakness. All I do is eat what my shaky teeth allow me to, and sleep, and entertain myself with my children and grandchildren when I need diversion."

"One can see from that how high you stand in the favor of heaven; I wish life were as kind to me!" said Liu *Lao-lao*.

The Matriarch was so charmed by the country simplicity and the ingenuity of her visitor that she promptly invited her to remain for a few days as her guest. Hsi-fêng saw to it that she had comfortable quarters.

(Kuhn, p. 252)

Having invited her to stay she also personally looks after her meals.

The Matriarch was glad to note her good appetite; she had heaping portions put before her and even gave her the best bits off her own plate.

(Kuhn, p. 255)

When the dancing performance was finished, the company rose from the table. The Matriarch took Liu *Lao-lao* by the hand and, making an extensive tour, showed her the remaining splendors of the Park of Delightful Vision [*Ta-kuan-yüan*].

(Kuhn, p. 258)

Besides this ability to show a somewhat unconventional amount of concern for a far from proper relative, she is a typical Chinese grandmother, devoted to her children and grandchildren, whom she believes have been given to her to train so as to bring honor and glory to the clan and to take care of their elders and respect their ancestors. But she is not contained in this training by the rigid standards of her son. She does not reject them, she simply stands apart from them when a higher priority intervenes. This freedom is clearly illustrated in one of the most dramatic scenes in the novel—Chia Cheng's beating of Pao-yü.

Chia Cheng rushed out, greatly agitated, to receive on the threshold the old lady who now entered, gasping and out of breath, supported by two maids and accompanied by a swarm of serving women.

"What drives my mother out into the open air in this heat? Why does she not order her son to come to her, if she has something to say to him?" asked Chia Cheng, bowing politely. The old *Tai tai* stood still, paused to take breath, and then said with an effort: "I would have had something to say, but as a good son has, alas, been denied to me, I do not really know to whom I could speak my mind."

Chia Cheng quickly fell to his knees.

"Your reproach grieves me beyond words, Mother. I have only given my son a lesson. I owed this to the memory of my glorious ancestors."

"Indeed? To beat to death—you call that a lesson? Did your father ever give you such lessons? . . ."

"You should have thought of me before you maltreated the poor boy so wickedly! You are a bad son. What do you want here? Do you want the further pleasure of looking on at his death? Get out of here! I do not wish to see you!" she rebuffed him indignantly.

(Kuhn, p. 243)

Her basic Confucian belief does not preclude a few Buddhist leanings also, although her earthy and pragmatic views belie any deep comm.cment to the basic philosophy of Buddhism that this world is largely an illusion and that reality lies beyond it. Lee Chen-tong has, I think, put his finger on the relationship of Buddhist philosophy to the lives of the Matriarch and most of the other women in the family.

Parmi les femmes de la noblesse le bouddhisme revêt une forme extériéure très luxueuse à cause de leurs richesses, mais manque totalement de vie intérieure, donc pour elles ce n'est qu'une question de cérémonies.[2]

The Matriarch communicates, therefore, a highly moral reality which stands outside of, but not in opposition to, dogma.

Despite her standing apart from it, however, she remains the center of a great deal of dogmatic structuring because of the conventions which surround her. The carefully prescribed behavior and rank at family gatherings, the daily *ch'ing-an* ritual, as well as the elaborate *kowtow*, with which inferiors in the family greet parents and superiors, the silent acceptance of humiliating rebuffs from her on the part of otherwise aggressive male leaders of the family, are all examples of actions structured by dogmatic Confucian principles. For instance, during the scene when the Matriarch is blaming Wang Fu-jen for plotting against her to take away her favorite maid, Yüan-yang, Wang Fu-jen is defenseless, because of the complexities of the rules governing proper action, to speak or to be spoken for.

Wang Fu-jen stood up and listened in silence, as it was not becoming for a daughter-in-law to defend herself when accused by her mother-in-law. Hsüeh Yi-ma, of course, could not say anything, as Wang Fu-jen was her sister. Li Huan and the others had left the room as soon as Yüan-yang began her recital of the story unfit for maidenly ears. Wang *Fu-jen*, guiltless as she was, stood and listened in silence.

T'an-ch'un comprehended Wang Fu-jen's difficult position. She realized that it was not for her to defend herself, nor for Hsüeh Yi-ma to defend her sister, nor for Pao-ch'ai to defend her aunt. It was also not fitting for Li Huan or Hsi-fêng or Pao-yü to speak. This was a time when daughters were needed. But Ying-ch'un lacked courage and Hsi-ch'un was too young. It was left to T'an-ch'un to speak out. She entered the room and smiled at the Matriarch.

(Wang, p. 306)

It is not easy to evaluate the effect of the report of such structured behavior upon the reading public of eighteenth-century China, and whether the author intended such restrictions to appear ludicrous or even undesirable. Probably not, since they would be comparable to numerous Victorian restrictions on the behavior of a proper young lady, which we fail to appreciate or tend to misinterpret today but which were a serious part of the English novel of the nineteenth century. Regardless of the interpretation of such scenes, however, the fact remains that dogmatic conventions were obviously responsible for structuring a good many of the actions of the characters, sometimes making it impossible for them to act on behalf of themselves or others and causing discomfort and unhappiness.

Confucian convention surely plays an essential part in the central tragedy of the story, the arrangement of Pao-yü's marriage. The personalities of the major figures and the motivations of the older members of the household, all formed by a system of Confucian convention, are the underlying cause of the tragedy. The prescribed customs which allowed Pao-yü's parents to control his marriage totally without consultation with him (thereby preventing him from declaring his choice and preventing Pao-ch'ai, as an intended bride, from communicating with her future husband until after the wedding ceremony) all compound to cause the circumstances of the tragedy.

Besides its role in defining the prescribed actions of filial and fraternal piety in the family, Confucianism also extends upward to outside authority and downward to include the proper modes of servants' behavior, as well as laterally, since it regulates all the basic social relationships. The behavior of the Chia family toward the Emperor and his representatives, the actions of their eldest daughter, the Imperial Concubine, during her visit at home, and their reception of her, are all in Chia Cheng's official government position minutely regulated by Confucian rules, as are his relationships with his superiors, his inferiors and his equals. Confucianism, therefore, permeates a major portion of the novel and controls a good part of the action.

A central question, of course, is the extent to which the *values* of Confucianism control the ideology of those whose external actions are controlled so closely by its *conventions,* and how much these same values control the moral view of the book. This is not an easily answered question, as we have seen, particularly because the dual authorship of the book has blurred its attitude toward Confucianism, and because the author was most probably constrained by political considerations from being too obvious in criticism of existing Confucian mores. In general, the novel, while accepting these values as the common working base of society, seems to reject them whenever they interfere with or contradict something spiritually or aesthetically higher, such as the love between Pao-yü and Tai-yü, or the belief in the spiritual transcendence of man; and a good portion of the novel, which focuses on another world beyond this one, and

[134]

which speaks of and illustrates the identity of nature with man (in the flowering begonia, for instance) is permeated with non-Confucian thought.

These non-Confucian, spiritual beliefs of Buddhism and Taoism are used frequently in the novel in parallel and sometimes intertwined ways. The pairing of the Buddhist monk and the Taoist priest in the opening section, for instance, as well as their later appearances together to point up the antithesis between the real and unreal worlds, and the acquiring of the twelve Buddhist nuns and the twelve Taoist priestesses to recite their respective liturgies at the time of the visit of the Imperial Concubine, indicate in the novel a link in function between the two beliefs. Some of their major metaphysical assumptions are blurred together—for instance, that the world is illusory and perfection lies in non-desire; that the condition of man is impermanent and suffering, and release lies in renunciation—often being referred to interchangeably, especially where they point to a life of solitude and contemplation as a refuge from the disillusionment and dissipation of the world. Also, since the religion of Taoism, as opposed to the metaphysics of Taoism, adopted many Buddhist ceremonial practices, references to the ritual of each are often difficult to separate.

Early in the novel, after the clearly Taoist exposition of the theme of artificiality versus non-artificiality in the opening chapter, specific references to the metaphysical assumptions of both Buddhism and Taoism are generally somewhat playful, often vaguely burlesqued. For instance, in the scene after Hsiang-yün has remarked that one of the actresses in the group that has just entertained looks like Tai-yü, Pao-yü, in his attempt to prevent her from saying this indelicate thing, has alienated both her and Tai-yü.

[135]

That is what I get for my good intention of trying to play the part of mediator between them! he thought to himself bitterly. Now I have fallen foul of both of them, and have to put up with reproaches from both sides. The wise Chuang-tzu was right when he said: "Why so much activity? It only gives one worry. Why trouble about all sorts of things? One is only annoyed by them. How splendid, on the other hand, only to care about one's own modest necessities of life, and so float on the waves free and alone as a boat adrift!" How useless is my striving and trouble! I do not even succeed in bringing about reconciliation and harmony between two girls! Why should I set myself higher aims?

(Kuhn, p. 169)

And he goes off to his room to lose himself in thoughts of Buddhist sadness of life.

Tears came to his eyes and he gave a loud sob. Then he got up, went to the writing table, took his brush, and worked off his ill-humor by writing a stanza full of the weariness of life and Buddhist renunciation of the world. Having done this, he felt more free and relieved, and lay down peacefully to sleep.

(Kuhn, p. 170)

Tai-yü, Pao-ch'ai and Hsiang-yün find the stanza the next morning and read it aloud.

> "Do what you want to! Come, go, as you please!
> Weep! Laugh! It's all the same to me.
> What do I care about the world!"

Thus read the stanza, the first part of which was written in the Sutra style.

"Oh, Cousin Pao-yü wants to join the saints and renounce the world!" the three of them cried, looking at each other with embarrassed smiles. Each of them felt a little bit guilty.

"Come, let us go to him together and bring him to reason!" suggested Tai-yü. And the three of them set off together to the

[136]

Chamber of the Fragrance of Culture. Tai-yü drew his attention to the fact that his Buddhist stanza was incomplete, and she added the missing conclusive point; and Pao-ch'ai mentioned the case of a well-known Buddhist sectarian who had resigned the leadership of his sect in favor of his cook, when the latter put him to shame by the correct criticism of a similarly defective stanza which he had composed. Pao-yü remarked with embarrassed astonishment that his clever cousins knew more than he himself did about a sphere which he had thought quite unknown to them. If they in spite of this did not presume to belong to the "awakened," he concluded that his chance of attaining to even a modest degree of holiness was positively nil. He therefore resigned himself to abandoning all idea of further striving after Buddhist contemplation.

"It was only a jest, the mood of a moment," he explained, smiling. And with this the happy old relationship between the cousins was restored.

(Kuhn, p. 170)

A later comment confirms this early tendency of Pao-yü's to be a Buddhist only at times of distress. One day he has gone over to see Tai-yü after an illness and finds her asleep and Tzǔ-chüan, her maid, sitting outside her room.

"How is your little mistress? Is her cough better?" he asked.
"Yes, thank you, it is a bit better."
"*A-mi-to-fo!* It's a relief to hear that."
"Since when do you invoke Buddha? That is something new to me!"
"Ah, well, in distress one clings to the doctor."

(Kuhn, p. 326)

As the story progresses, however, and particularly after the loss of his jade, his marriage with Pao-ch'ai and the death of Tai-yü, Pao-yü becomes seriously and intellectually interested in what before was for him more of a negative distraction than an affirmative belief. He begins to probe more deeply into philosophy, particularly into the writings of Chuang-tzu and the Taoists concerning the relationship of man and nature, and the philosophy of non-action and non-desire.

> After his recovery Pao-yü showed himself extraordinarily changed in character as compared with his former self. He was silent and wrapt in meditation; he buried himself in his books, mostly of Taoist literature, avoided conversation and company, and—a fact which was particularly remarked with much shaking of heads—paid no more attention to his feminine environment.
>
> (Kuhn, p. 569)

He is drawn more and more to a desire for renunciation, which he expresses in Buddhist terms, another example of the blurring of the two ways of life as a means of refuge from the world.

> "Have you no feeling for your parents, who are suffering so much on your account? Pull yourself together and reward their love by achieving something noble."
> "Oh, is what I intimated not a noble achievement? Do you not know the saying:
>
> > "A son who to the Buddha vows his life
> > Opens heaven's gate to seven ancestors."
> >
> > (Kuhn, p. 574)

And after Hsi-ch'un has won agreement from her family allowing her to become a solitary in the Kingfisher's Cave, Pao-yü makes reference, in Buddhist terms, to his similar longing.

> When Hsi-ch'un bade farewell to the family everyone expected that Pao-yü would get another of his bad turns and raise a passionate lament over the new loss of a little sister, but to everyone's surprise he remained quite calm this time.

[138]

"*A-mi-to-fo!* you have done it! What a pity that I am not ready yet!" These were all the words of farewell that he said.

(Kuhn, p. 575)

At the same time it becomes increasingly clear that the naturally Taoist outlook of the aesthetically sensitive Pao-yü is being more and more confirmed by his serious intellectual contact with its beliefs, and that this synthesis, plus the sad circumstances of his life, justified by the metaphysical pessimism of Buddhism, have combined to turn him religiously and philosophically toward a way of life transcending his earlier involvement and sympathy with those around him.

Since Pao-yü is the central consciousness of the book, his decision embodies the central moral dimension of the novel, a rejection of this world in favor of the non-world of the Great Void. It is a symmetrically satisfying action which superimposes his developed, photographic image on the negative outlined in the supernatural portions to find that they correspond.

The novel, however, communicates through its innumerable pages the goodness of material things—of food, of happy company, of conversation and poetry writing, of nature—and the simple relish of these things is so strongly pervasive a theme that it is not simply negated by Pao-yü's gradual retreat from and final rejection of them. Though the reader follows the increasing momentum of the family's decline, Hsi-fêng's disintegration and the sad sequence of Pao-yü's forced and unhappy marriage, and laments these things as illustrative of the evils of the Red Dust, he does not equate them with the simple condition of living in the artificial world of earth, but with living there selfishly and without concern for others. Therefore, while the rejection of the goods of the world as well as its evils, which is included in Pao-yü's decision and the attitude of acceptance and inevitability of that decision on the part of his father and the others, represents the stated moral theme of the book, it is softened and diffused by the contrasting and brilliant picture which the reader retains of the worldly delights as morally good.

Perhaps this imbalance in the theme of the book is a built-in imbalance in life—it is easier to see and evaluate and be moved by the tangible realities of both good and evil in this world than by the intangible realities of the world beyond. Ts'ao Hsüeh-ch'in tried to conquer this problem by making the world of the Great Void as tangible and particular as possible, but the magnetism of the known and experienced, which is desirable simply because it is familiar, was too great to make him totally successful.

The conflict between the stated theme of other-worldliness and the implied appeal of this-worldliness arises, too, perhaps because *The Dream of the Red Chamber* is not basically a religious or philosophical novel. Its emphasis is on the characters and their actions and reactions, and the element of spirituality dominates only through their absorption of Buddhist and Taoist thought and their resultant acts and attitudes, and not through philosophical speculation or metaphysical debate. Because of this emphasis on "lived" ideas, the fine distinctions of dogma and philosophy are often blurred when they emerge through the medium of the characters' lives, because they carry with them not only the clear assent of their minds, but the indistinct agglomeration of their emotions and feelings. While this dims somewhat the moral pattern that the book presents, it represents once more the strong particularity and immediacy of the novel, which communicates the complexities of life more than it criticizes it.

Various other aspects of Buddhism and Taoism show

up in the novel in a number of ways. An example is their appearance as a particular kind of religious force in the life of Miao-yü, the young Buddhist nun living a life of contemplation in a little hermitage on the edge of the Chia compound, or in Shih-yin, the squire of Soochow who, early in the book, renounces the world for a life of Taoist contemplation and then reappears again at the end to complete the story. The story of Miao-yü is particularly interesting because it is the only sequence in which renunciation of the world is shown to be a dedicated struggle against worldly desires and not simply an easy refuge from worldly evils. She is proud and aristocratic and aloof and her struggle with the demons of fleshly temptation is intense. This struggle is memorably illustrated in a scene which begins one evening when Pao-yü stops to visit Hsi-ch'un and finds Miao-yü with her playing chess. The surprise of his presence forces Miao-yü to return to her hermitage immediately.

"It's time for me to go. I have already stayed too long," said Miao-yü, anticipating him; she rose and turned towards the door.

"I only hope I shall not lose my way. I'm so unfamiliar with this labyrinth of winding paths," she remarked with a smile as she reached the door, glancing aside at Pao-yü. He read a silent invitation in her glance.

"I will guide you," he offered promptly.

"Oh, how very kind of you. Then please walk ahead!"

And the beautiful and saintly lady gladly allowed the scion of princes, a child from the world of red dust, to guide her back to her hermitage by winding paths.

That night she had to go through a bitter fight with the demons of temptation. After she had taken her frugal evening meal, burned incense, prayed through her daily Sutra breviary, and had sat down with her legs tucked crosswise under her on her round prayer cushion, she sought in vain, for several hours of strenuous meditation, to banish all frivolous, worldly thoughts and to achieve the prescribed inner peace pleasing to God. . . . The demons of temptation entered into her body and dangled fleshly visions before her. At first these took the form of high-born and high-spirited youths who wooed her and whom she proudly scorned; female marriage brokers scrambled for possession of her and tried to drag her into a bridal litter; and finally she saw herself as the booty of robbers, who dragged her away and were about to violate her. Bathed in sweat, foaming at the mouth, with outspread hands and staring eyes, she awoke from her ecstasy. For days she lay in a semi-conscious state until, by dint of swallowing quantities of medicines which the doctor prescribed "for the cooling of the fire in the blood," she finally recovered.

(Kuhn p. 455)

If we see this struggle as representative of the difficulty of transcending the world while remaining in it, however, it is perhaps a clear affirmation of the wisdom of Pao-yü's final choice in his total rejection of the world, a choice already presaged and mirrored in that of Shih-yin.

The Dream of the Red Chamber is an iridescent book. As it moves, it sends flashes of light from various incidents and characters in a varicolored pattern, depending on the angle or the distance at any given moment. The broad moral dimensions of the story are controlled by Taoist and Buddhist metaphysics and spiritual beliefs, particularly the Taoist standard of non-artificiality and spontaneity, which lead the characters from the transcendent plane of reality at the beginning, through the valley of unreality, back to the transcendent plane at the end. Local incidents, characters and actions, however, are often controlled by an involvement in the good things of this world or by Confucian interests in social dimensions, and there is an implied this-worldly appeal which forms a tension in the physiognomy and atmosphere of the story which emphasizes the confusion and complexity of life at the expense of a clear moral pattern. There are numerous forces which contribute to this complexity: the background of Chinese life itself, which is informed by these same conflicting and contradictory streams of dogma and belief; the episodic nature of the novel which tends to be unfastidiously inclusive and unconcerned about contradictions; and the concern with bringing alive the individuals who people the novel no matter how they take their place in it. If we agree with Dorothy Van Ghent that we must judge a novel "by the cogency and illuminative quality of the view of life that it affords,"[3] and with Barbara Hardy that, "In telling his story, or in between telling his story, the novelist is also organizing his criticism of life,"[4] we must judge *The Dream of the Red Chamber* as lacking in an overall, definable moral and aesthetic pattern which would provide this view.

Looking back over our previous analysis of the structural elements of the novel, however, we can see that it is a book which, while it sprawls over the limits of a properly organized pattern, remains nevertheless vitally alive. For the beauty of this enormous work lies in its richness and variety of characterization, combined with its quiet flow of movement and detailed texture.

Afterword

THE *Dream of the Red Chamber* can be endlessly read, interpreted, and reinterpreted. Its popularity continues on many planes. Its characters and scenes are familiar in traditional Peking opera productions, and it is studied by modern-day Maoists in Communist China. Yet, in general, the critical approaches of the past have been essentially nonaesthetic in tone, aimed at establishing historical, sociological or political truths, rather than "the truth of life."

Mention has been made earlier of the attempts to establish the novel as autobiographical and the great deal of research that has gone into discovering the details of Ts'ao Hsüeh-ch'in's life in order to illuminate the sources of the book. Yet from an artistic point of view this approach, while interesting, is of little value and the small amount of material available concerning Ts'ao Hsüeh-ch'in's life has added little to the interior dimensions of the novel. C. T. Hsia notes that ". . . even today we know fewer biographical facts about Ts'ao Hsüeh-ch'in than about Shakespeare, and of the many girls in his life, whose importance in the novel had prompted the commentator to provide the headnote, we know practically nothing beyond what we may infer from the commentary."[1]

Also, the search for autobiographical clues has become a two-edged sword, since some writers have attempted to build a biographical sketch of the author from the incidents and relationships in the novel, as well as to find in his life story hints that would make the novel more understandable. This attempt to read the novel as autobiography has been warned against clearly, by Liu Wu-chi and by Wu Shih-ch'ang:

The novel itself, because of its partly autobiographical nature, provides some clues to the earlier part of the life of the author. But as it is, after all, a fiction, or the story of the "Chia" (fictitious) family and the "true facts are hidden" (chên-shih yin), these clues, unless correlated with Chih-yen's commentary and other relevant material, are more deceptive than reliable. It calls for the utmost caution if facts are to be deduced from the novel.[2]

Earlier "critics" and scholars searched for the hidden true stories that the novel was supposed to contain— romantic stories of an emperor and his favorite courtesan or of a poet and his concubine. The very particularity of the setting and the characters encouraged attempts to search out realities that underlay it as such lifelikeness was hard to accept as pure fiction. This approach, which fails to emphasize the value of the novel as literature, is not basically critical in tone.

Throughout the years there has been a tendency, increased recently, to analyze the novel in sociological and/ or political terms as—variously—a critique of the examination system, the legal system, the marriage and joint family system, the general underlying Confucian values of most periods of Chinese history, or as an attack on the Manchu dynasty. Anti-Confucian Maoists, delving into this novel, find it easy to draw simplified parallels between Chia Cheng and a provincial or national magistrate of similar ineptness, or between Wang Hsi-fêng and a similarly unscrupulous person who professes all the external virtues of proper Confucian behavior. At the other extreme, traditional Confucian critics have sometimes used the book to illustrate the weaknesses of those who profess to be good Confucians when indeed they are not, condemning the practitioners, therefore, instead of the system.[3]

Yet, despite these many and varied approaches to the novel, it has never been thoroughly evaluated in *purely* aesthetic and artistic terms by either Chinese or Western critics. The most extensive piece of recent criticism in English is by C. T. Hsia, who, in his volume on the classic Chinese novel, devotes a chapter to a discussion of *The Dream of the Red Chamber*. He reviews what we know of the composition of the novel, emphasizes the basic unity of the work, identifying Kao Ê as editor—not author—of the last forty chapters, then analyzes the three characters in the romantic plot (Pao-yü, Tai-yü, and Pao-ch'ai) in the light of the underlying philosophy of the novel and the central tension shown there between compassion and personal salvation. In this connection he points to the recurring contrast between love and lust:

The schematic presentation of love and lust in the novel, therefore, runs to this formula: those sunk in the mire of gross passions (with the exception of Chia Yü-ts'un, the vulgar and unscrupulous official whose importance in the allegorical scheme entitles him to a final encounter with Taoist wisdom) make no attempt to extricate themselves, while those whose love, given the chance to blossom, could have seriously challenged the ideal of renunciation and represented another kind of fulfillment (and the author's sympathy fully entitles us to this expectation) are systematically destroyed so as to leave room for the Buddhist-Taoist moral.[4]

and from another angle:

Whereas in other cultures adolescents rush into adulthood to embrace the challenges of marriage and work, these maidens, while also preoccupied with love and anxious for their future, want at the same time to prolong indefinitely their age of innocence, fearful to step into the realm of experience. With all the examples of unhappy women around them, experience means for them primarily the sexual assault upon their child-hood placidity, with all its implied consequences of corruption and unhappiness.[5]

This analysis is in keeping with Hsia's contention that the "unavoidable tragedy resides solely in the clash be-tween the opposing claims of love and personal libera-tion. So overpowering, indeed, is the sense of tragedy implicit in his ordeal that, in choosing to renounce the world, Pao-yü may be said to have embraced an illusion of far less substantial weave than the human cloth of love and compassion. . . ."[6] Whether one believes this to be the central conflict of the novel or not, Hsia makes a con-vincing argument for its presence there, and provides a framework of interpretation within which a portion of the novel can be placed and judged. He does not, how-ever, attempt to analyze the entire novel, nor to draw a plan for criticism which would include such important elements as, for instance, the increasing complexity of Wang Hsi-fêng's manipulations or the rise and fall of the Chia clan.

Other critical comments on the novel are contained in the chapters on Ch'ing fiction found in the basic English histories of Chinese literature, the best of them by Chen Shou-yi, Liu Wu-chi, Lu Hsün, and Lai Ming. Each of these works is worth consulting for the overall impres-sion that it gives of the book; none makes an extensive or particularly original analysis of the novel, the purpose of all of them being primarily introductory rather than critical.

The novel's great strength lies in its ability to speak to people about people in all times and all places. Pao-yü, for instance, is not simply a weak, effeminate creature, cowed by a Confucian father and spoiled by a dominant grandmother. He is a complex, sensitive human being trying his best to work out his life in terms of what he knows of reality and unreality—a person with whom many readers can identify in spite of the very special cultural circumstances in which he is imbedded. So with Tai-yü, Pao-ch'ai, Wang Hsi-fêng and a host of others. They exceed their specifically Chinese characteristics and, as they make their way to The Great Void Illusion Land, or Heaven, exist in the common world of fictional human beings.

Great novels of all times have produced persons who, transcending their origins in fiction, rival eminent "historical" figures (past and present) in shaping our thinking. A major contribution of *The Dream of the Red Chamber* is the individuality and strength of the people it has introduced to this teeming universe. There is little doubt that these persons have exercised a very real influence in the course of history and that their lives and personalities must be taken into consideration in any attempt to understand the rich and many-faceted cultures of the world.

Works Consulted

Allott, Miriam. *Novelists on the Novel.* New York: Columbia University Press, 1959.

Ames, Van Meter. *Aesthetics of the Novel.* Chicago: University of Chicago Press, 1928.

Auerbach, Erich. *Mimesis.* Princeton, N.J.: Princeton University Press, 1953.

Booth, Wayne C. *The Rhetoric of Fiction.* Chicago: University of Chicago Press, 1961.

Brown, E. K. *Rhythm in the Novel.* Toronto: University of Toronto Press, 1950.

Ch'en Shou-yi. *Chinese Literature, A Historical Introduction.* New York: Ronald Press, 1961. A general introduction to the field of Chinese literature by periods and genres. A wide overview, filled with detail, which sometimes loses the reader in a maze of information. Includes some translated selections as illustrations.

Chou Shu-jen (Lu Hsun). *A Brief History of Chinese Fiction.* Peking: Foreign Languages Press, 1959. A quick and standard survey of Chinese fiction. Includes summaries and evaluations of novels by this well-known 20th century Chinese novelist.

de Bary, William Theodore, Wing-tsit Chan, and Burton Watson, eds. *Sources of Chinese Tradition.* New York: Columbia University Press, 1960. A collection of source materials in Chinese culture and intellectual history with helpful introductory material. Brings together a good deal of hard-to-find material in good translations.

Forster, E. M. *Aspects of the Novel.* New York: Harcourt Brace, 1927.

Frye, Northrop. *Anatomy of Criticism.* Princeton: Princeton University Press, 1957.

Fung Yu-lan. *A Short History of Chinese Philosophy.* Edited by Derk Bodde. New York: Macmillan, 1948.

Hardy, Barbara. *The Appropriate Form.* London: Athlone Press, 1964.

Horne, Charles. *The Technique of the Novel.* New York: Harper, 1908.

Hsia, C. T. *The Classic Chinese Novel.* New York: Columbia University Press, 1968. A very readable and helpful analysis in depth of the six classic Chinese novels by one of the best of the contemporary Chinese critics.

————. "Love and Compassion in 'Dream of the Red Chamber.'" *Criticism* V (Summer, 1963): 261–71. A discussion of the central conflict facing Pao-yü in the novel and the relationship between love and compassion as forces in his decision.

————. " 'On The Red Chamber Dream' by Wu Shih-ch'ang." Reviewed in *Journal of Asian Studies* XXI (Nov., 1961): 78–80.

Hugo, Howard E., ed. *Aspects of Fiction, A Handbook.* Boston: Little, 1962.

'Hung Lou Meng' Jen Ming Tzu Tien (紅樓夢人名辭典). Hongkong: n.d. A brief annotation of each of the characters of the *Hung Lou Meng.*

James, Henry. *The Art of Fiction and Other Essays.* Edited and introduction by Morris Roberts. Toronto: Oxford, 1947.

————. *The Art of the Novel.* Edited and introduction by R. P. Blackmur. London: Scribner, 1950.

————. *Notes on Novelists.* London: Scribner, 1914.

————. *Partial Portraits.* London: Macmillan, 1911.

Kou Lin-ke. *Essai sur le Hong Leou Mong (Le Rêve dans le Pavillon Rouge).* Thèse pour le doctorat, Université de Lyon, 1935.

Kuhn, Franz, trans. *Der Traum der roten Kammer.* Leipzig: Insel-Verlag, 1932. (*See below:* McHugh, Florence and Isabel.)

Lee Ghen-tong. *Étude sur Le Songe du Pavillon Rouge.* Thèse pour le doctorat, Université de Paris, 1934.

Liddell, Robert. *Some Principles of Fiction.* Bloomington: Indiana University Press, 1954.

————. *A Treatise on the Novel.* London: Jonathan Cape, 1953.

Lin Yu-t'ang (林語堂). "Reopening the Question of Authorship of 'Red Chamber Dream' " (平心論高鶚). *Bulletin of the Institute of History and Philology, Academia Sinica* XXIX (Nov., 1958): 327–87.

Liu Wu-chi. *An Introduction to Chinese Literature.* Bloomington: Indiana University Press, 1966. Probably the best of the introductions to Chinese literature because it synthesizes detail and provides a clear historical framework.

Lu Yueh Hwa. *La Jeune Fille Chinoise d'après Hong-Leou-Mong.* Thèse pour le doctorat, Université de Paris, 1936.

Lubbock, Percy. *The Craft of Fiction.* London: Jonathan Cape, 1921.

Macauley, Robie, and George Lanning. *Technique in Fiction.* New York: Harper, 1964.

McHugh, Florence and Isabel, trans. *The Dream of the Red Chamber.* Introduction by Franz Kuhn. New York: Pantheon Books, 1958. A translation of most of the *Dream of the Red Chamber* from the German text of Franz Kuhn. The translators retain much of the detail of individual scenes but choose among the scenes to be translated. Sometimes awkward, but retains an authentic feel of the original.

McKillop, Alan Dugald. *The Early Masters of English Fiction.* Lawrence, Kansas: University of Kansas Press, 1962.

Muir, Edwin. *The Structure of the Novel.* New York: Harcourt, 1929.

O'Connor, Frank. *The Mirror in the Roadway.* New York: Knopf, 1956.

O'Connor, William Van. *Forms of Modern Fiction.* Minneapolis: University of Minnesota Press, 1948.

Rexroth, Kenneth. "Classics Revisited—XXI—'Dream of the Red Chamber.'" *Saturday Review,* Jan. 1, 1966, p. 19.

Reischauer, Edwin O., and John K. Fairbank. *East Asia, The Great Tradition.* Boston: Houghton, 1960.

Santayana, George. *Essays in Literary Criticism.* Edited by Irving Singer. New York: Scribner, 1956.

Scholes, Robert, ed. *Approaches to the Novel.* San Francisco: Chandler, 1961.

Shapiro, Charles. *Twelve Original Essays on Great English Novels.* Detroit: Wayne State University Press, 1960.

Spence, Jonathan D. *Ts'ao Yin and the K'ang-hsi Emperor: Bondservant and Master.* New Haven: Yale University Press, 1966.

Tolstoi, Lyof. N. *The Complete Works, Vol. I.* New York: Crowell, 1927.

Ts'ao Hsüeh-ch'in (曹雪芹). *Hung Lou Meng* (紅樓夢), 2 vols. Hongkong, n.d. The most readily available Chinese version of the novel in 120 chapters, published in Hong Kong.

Van Ghent, Dorothy. *The English Novel, Form and Function*. New York: Rinehart, 1953.

Wang, Chi-chen, trans. *Dream of the Red Chamber*. Preface by Mark Van Doren. New York: Twayne Publishers, 1958. Most recent translation of *The Dream of the Red Chamber* from the original Chinese by a respected Chinese-American scholar. The translation attempts a kind of colloquial English that brings the novel to the American reader but loses some of the original flavor.

Watt, Ian. *The Rise of the Novel*. Berkeley: University of California Press, 1964.

West, Anthony. "Through a Glass Darkly." *The New Yorker*, Nov. 22, 1958.

Wharton, Edith. *The Writing of Fiction*. New York: Scribner, 1925.

Wu Shih-ch'ang. *On The Red Chamber Dream*. Oxford: Clarendon Press, 1961. An excellent and readable discussion of the many textual problems involved in identifying the authentic script of the novel and the varying points of view concerning its authorship.

Notes

CHAPTER I. INTRODUCTION

1. "Chia" means "false."

2. Actually Professor Wang made two separate translations, as he states in a prefatory note to the latter. In the 1929 translation he took the novel to be a love story and omitted several scenes which seemed to him, then, to be trivial details. Later he altered his opinion, deciding that many of these episodes contributed to the novel as the chronicle of a family. The 1958 edition retains much more of the first eighty chapters, which he judges to be the original, using only about one-tenth of the Kao Ê contribution which completes the novel.

3. For further discussion see C. T. Hsia, Review of *"On The Red Chamber Dream* by Wu Shih-ch'ang," *Journal of Asian Studies* XXI (November, 1961): 78–80; and Lin Yu-t'ang, "Reopening the Question of Authorship of 'Red Chamber Dream,' " *Academia Sinica* XXIX (November, 1958): 327–87.

4. See Chapter 9 in Kenneth Scott Latourette, *The Chinese; Their History and Culture,* 4th ed. (New York: The Macmillan Company, 1964).

5. An historical analogy is the 1890's in American society when the *nouveau riche* "robber barons" spent fortunes on clothing from Paris, castles imported or custom-built on the Great Lakes, and debutante parties for thousands of people.

6. C. T. Hsia, *The Classic Chinese Novel* (New York: Columbia University Press, 1968), pp. 10–11.

7. Liu Wu-chi, *An Introduction to Chinese Literature* (Bloomington, Ind.: Indiana University Press, 1966), pp. 202–203.

8. Percy Lubbock, *The Craft of Fiction* (London: Jonathan Cape, 1921), p. 41.

9. Barbara Hardy, *The Appropriate Form* (London: Athlone Press, 1964), pp. 1–2

10. E. M. Forster, *Aspects of the Novel* (New York: Harcourt Brace, 1927), p. 26.

11. Ibid., p. 27.

12. Richard Crane, "The Concept of Plot." In *Approaches to the Novel* edited by Robert Scholes (San Francisco: Chandler, 1961), p. 160.

13. Ibid., p. 165.

14. Dorothy Van Ghent, *The English Novel: Form and Function* (New York: Rinehart, 1953), p. 65.

15. Leo Tolstoy quoted in Miriam Allott, *Novelists on the Novel* (New York: Columbia University Press, 1959), p. 235.

16. Norman Friedman, "Point of View in Fiction: The Development of a Critical Concept." In *Approaches to the Novel*, p. 136.

17. Forster, p. 88.

18. Hardy, p. 13.

19. Northrop Frye, *The Anatomy of Criticism* (Princeton, N. J.: Princeton University Press, 1957), p. 11.

20. Forster, p. 24.

21. Ian Watt, *The Rise of the Novel* (Berkeley: University of California Press, 1964), p. 32.

22. Van Ghent, pp. 3–4.

23. Watt, p. 15.

24. Joyce Cary in *Aspects of Fiction*, edited by Howard E. Hugo (Boston: Little, 1962), p. 224.

25. Quoted in Hardy, p. 33.

26. Forster, p. 94.

27. Crane, pp. 165–166.

28. Elizabeth Bowen in *Aspects of Fiction*, p. 179.

29. Hardy, pp. 138–139.

CHAPTER 2. NARRATIVE STYLE

1. For example, in the pantomime which precedes the play acted in *Hamlet*.

2. In Kuhn edition, the "Guardian of the Radiance of the Stone of the Gods" and the "Purple Pearl."

3. The "dream of the red chamber" from which the novel takes its name. "Hung-lou" or "red chamber" refers to women's quarters.

4. References will be made to the Hong-Kong edition of the text (*Hung Lou Meng*, 2 vols., n.d.).

5. The family is prosperous, but they are consuming wildly beyond their means.

6. The plural is used to suggest that the speakers are the priest and the monk.

7. This device is well known to audiences of the American soap-opera.

8. These values, honor of family and education, are fundamental to Confucian teaching.

CHAPTER 3. CHARACTERS

1. The Japanese *wabi*, frequently used by Bashō, the greatest Haiku poet, defines this tendency "to be sorrowful, to feel the transiency of the world, . . . to be lonely, to feel there is nothing to rely on."

2. Hsia, "Love and Compassion," Criticism V (summer, 1963), pp. 268–269.

3. This relates to a point made by Robert Liddell in *A Treatise on the Novel* (London: Jonathan Cape, 1953), p. 60": . . . the important thing to discover about the novelist is not chiefly what characters he thinks good, but rather what characters he thinks 'nice' . . .," a sublety that depends greatly on the modes and manners of a given period of fiction. The implication is that the objective goodness or badness of a character, as measured against the ethics or dogma of the time, is not the only test of the moral use of character.

4. Edwin Muir, *The Structure of the Novel* (New York: Harcourt, 1929),p. 84.

5. Hsia, "Love and Compassion," p. 262.

CHAPTER 4. TIME AND SPACE IN THE NOVEL

1. Muir, pp. 62–63.

2. Ibid., pp. 59–60.

3. Forster, p. 29.

4. Ibid., p. 28.

5. Balzac quoted in Allott, p. 303.

6. Muir, p. 65.

7. Austin Warren, "Nature and Modes of Narrative Fiction." In *Approaches to the Novel*, p. 202.

8. Elizabeth Bowen in *Aspects of Fiction*, p. 187.

9. Percy Lubbock, *The Craft of Fiction* (London: Jonathan Cape, 1921), p. 49.

10. Warren, p. 199.

11. Lubbock, p. 109.

12. E. K. Brown, *Rhythm in the Novel* (Toronto: University of Toronto Press, 1950), pp. 17–18.

13. Ibid., p. 9.

14. Forster, p. 167.

15. Van Ghent, p. 68.

16. Ibid., p. 15.

17. Lubbock, p. 45.

CHAPTER 5. MORAL VIEW AS A CONTROLLING FORCE

1. Fung Yu-lan, *A Short History of Chinese Philosophy* (New York: The Macmillan Company, 1964), p. 78.

2. Lee Ghen-tong, *Étude sur Le Songe du Pavillon Rouge* (Thèse pour le doctorat, Université de Paris, 1934), p. 101.

3. Van Ghent, p. 7.

4. Hardy, p. 2.

AFTERWORD

1. C. T. Hsia, *The Classic Chinese Novel*, p. 247.
2. Wu Shih-ch'ang, *On The Red Chamber Dream* (Oxford: Clarendon Press, 1961), p. 114.
3. Liu (p. 237) neatly summarizes this vast range of critical interpretation.
4. Hsia, *The Classic Chinese Novel*, p. 265.
5. Ibid., p. 280.
6. Ibid., p. 296–297.

CHECKLIST OF FEMALE NAMES

Wade-Giles *Romanization*	*Kuhn (McHugh)* *translation*	*Wang translation*
Chih Neng	Chi Neng	Chih-neng *or* Neng-erh
Chin Ke	King Kuo	Kin-kue
Ch'in K'e-ch'ing	Chin Ko Ching	Chin-shih
Chin-kuei	Golden Cinnamon	Cassia
Ch'ing-wen	Bright Cloud	Bright Design *or* Ching-wen
Hsi-ch'un	Grief of Spring	Compassion Spring or Hsi-chun
Hsi-fêng	Phoenix	Phoenix *or* Feng-chieh
Hsi-jên	Pearl	Pervading Fragrance *or* Hsi-jen
Hsiang-yün	Little Cloud	River Mist or Yun Ya-tou
Hsüeh Yi-ma	Aunt Hsueh	Aunt Hsueh *or* Hsueh *Yi-ma*
Liu *Lao-lao*	Grandmother Liu	Liu *Lao-lao*
Miao-yü	Miao-yu	(does not appear)
Pao-ch'ai	Precious Clasp	Precious Virtue *or* Pao Chieh-chieh
Pao-ch'in	Precious Harp	Precious Harp
P'ing-erh	Little Ping	Patience *or* Ping-erh
Tai-yü	Black Jade	Black Jade *or* Lin Tai-yu
T'an-ch'un	Taste of Spring	Quest Spring *or* Tan-chun
Tzŭ-chüan	Cuckoo	Purple Cuckoo or Tzu-chuan
Wang Fu-jen	Madame Cheng	Madame Wang
Yu Erh-chieh	Second Sister Yu	Yu Erh-chieh
Yu San-chieh	Third Sister Yu	Yu San-chieh
Yüan-ch'un	Beginning of Spring	Cardinal Spring
Yüan-yang	Mandarin Duck	Faith

NOTE For purposes of clarity I have consistently used the title Matriarch for Pao-yü's grandmother, in quoted passages as well as in my own text. She appears in the Kuhn translation as the Ancestress and in the Wang translation both as the Matriarch and as Lao *Tai-tai*. However, when in dialogue one of the characters refers to her as *Tai-tai* I have let it stand as a familiar mode of address.

Index of Characters